Praise for *The Millionaire Maker's*
Guide to Creating a Cash Machine for Life

"When rich people get together they don't talk about saving money; they talk about the other side of the ledger, how to make money with money. They talk about all sorts of businesses they are into to augment their paycheck and create even more wealth.

"Yet, the vast majority of financial self-help books are all about trying to make ends meet, about trying to take a little bit of money and conserve it. Some might focus on how to invest better in the stock market. But almost none talk about what the wealthy talk about when they chat: making big money on the money they have.

"Loral's book may be the first I have read that doesn't patronize you or try to keep you from making the big money I know you have the ability to make with some help, help from Loral. She, like me, doesn't make it 'easy' and 'simple.' She shows the hard work these efforts take. But do not be discouraged; she will get you there.

"You want to keep up with the Joneses, be my guest. You want to trounce the Joneses and the rest of the gang? Don't just read this book, act on it."
—James J. Cramer, CBNC's *Mad Money* and TheStreet.com

"I have known Loral for years; since she had a JOB . . . today she is worth many millions and she sure can create Cash Machines. If you want to become a Millionaire, do exactly what Loral tells you . . . *everyone* who does earns a lot of money; believe me, I have watched it happen."
—Bob Proctor
author of the bestseller *You Were Born Rich;*
"philosopher" of *The Secret*

"Loral Langemeier teaches people to think differently—beyond the traditional—about their money and guides them on a path to greater wealth. This book is a very practical guide for those looking to launch their own businesses while keeping their day jobs!"
—John Gray
best-selling author of *Men Are from Mars, Women Are from Venus*

"Loral Langemeier has developed a terrific cash machine herself. I can't think of a better person to write this book. *The Millionaire Maker's Guide to Creating a Cash Machine for Life* is a practical guide for those thinking of starting a business. It provides a no-nonsense approach to the skills necessary for budding entrepreneurs and gives good tips on developing profitable business concepts."
—Sandy Botkin CPA, Esq.
president, Tax Reduction Institute;
author of *Lower Your Taxes: BIG TIME* and *Real Estate Tax Secrets of the Rich*

"What a breath of fresh air. Instead of promising short-term instant success and millions by next week, Loral's *Cash Machine for Life* lays a comprehensive step-by-step foundation for wealth you can put in the bank, year after year after year."
—Paul Lemberg
CEO and chief business accelerator, Quantum Growth Consulting;
author of *Be Unreasonable. The Unconventional Way to Extraordinary Business Results*

"What's better than an enormous pile of cash sitting right in front of you? Answer: A cash machine that can continue to generate piles of cash for you. Loral Langemeier has created one for you with her new and exciting book, *The Millionaire Maker's Guide to Creating a Cash Machine for Life*. You're going to love both the book and the cash."
—Jay Conrad Levinson, the Father of Guerrilla Marketing;
author of the *Guerrilla Marketing* series of books

"WOW! Another classic must read book for anyone serious about achieving the dream of total financial freedom. Loral has the unique ability to take you by the hand and show you how real wealth is created by average people. She blows away all of the myths you have been taught about success and real wealth accumulation."
—Brian Sacks, nationally renowned mortgage and marketing expert,
founder of www.glazer-kennedywebstore.com
and www.loanofficersuccess.com;
author of the bestseller *Yes You Can Get a Mortgage*

"I've watched Loral do a 'money-makeover' and in ten minutes show people six better ways to make money with assets they don't even realize they have. Her skills are original, unique and, from what I've seen, unmatched, when it comes to maximizing and building wealth."
—Chet Holmes
author of *The Ultimate Sales Machine;*
advisor to more than 60 of the Fortune 500

THE
MILLIONAIRE MAKER'S GUIDE
TO
CREATING A CASH MACHINE FOR LIFE

THE
MILLIONAIRE
MAKER'S GUIDE
TO
CREATING A
CASH MACHINE
FOR LIFE

Loral Langemeier

McGraw-Hill

New York   Chicago   San Francisco
Lisbon   London   Madrid   Mexico City   Milan
New Delhi   San Juan   Seoul   Singapore
Sydney   Toronto

2 3 4 5 6 7 8 9 0   DOC/DOC   0 9 8 7

ISBN-13: 978–0–07–148473–2
ISBN-10:   0–07–148473–6

This publication is designed to provide accurate and authoritative information in regard to the subject matter covered. It is sold with the understanding that neither the author nor the publisher is engaged in rendering legal, accounting, or other professional service. If legal advice or other expert assistance is required, the services of a competent professional person should be sought.

> —*From a Declaration of Principles jointly adopted*
> *by a Committee of the American Bar*
> *Association and a Committee of Publishers*

Cash Machine, Financial Freedom Day, Gap Analysis, and Wealth Account are trademarks of Choice Performance, Inc.

McGraw-Hill books are available at special quantity discounts to use as premiums and sales promotions, or for use in corporate training programs. For more information, please write to the Director of Special Sales, Professional Publishing, McGraw-Hill, Two Penn Plaza, New York, NY 10121–2298. Or contact your local bookstore.

This book is printed on acid-free paper.

*To my dad, who gave me strength, endurance, and the capacity
to do what I do. I miss you—you left us far too soon.*

Contents

Foreword

At the beginning of a new company, most inexperienced entrepreneurs find themselves woefully alone. Oh, there's family, yes, and friends. But most often, family and friends give would-be entrepreneurs the advice they want to hear, as opposed to the advice they need to hear if the company they want to create stands any chance of success.

And, of course, most companies don't succeed. Most new businesses do fail, not necessarily because there was anything wrong with the business idea but because the knowledge of what to do and how to do it is so transparently absent.

This book provides any new business owner with exactly what's needed to begin the process—wonderfully rich and useful stories about how others approached the opportunity to create their "Cash Machine" and pulled it off.

- What do you do when it seems like nothing is working?
- What do you take solace in when you're all alone?

- Whom do you go to for examples of ordinary people doing extraordinary things to get their businesses off the ground?
- How do you even *think* about this leap you're about to take, unless it is to read academic business books that don't really speak to you as a friend and "Dutch uncle" would?

Loral is that friend and Dutch uncle everyone needs when feeling alone.

She knows of what she speaks. Loral is a remarkably energetic and passionate woman who has done all she writes about on her own and has succeeded splendidly in a game in which very few win. Loral writes from the heart, delivers her good news from the head, and brings the two together—head and heart—in a way guaranteed to touch you, dear readers, with the most important message of our time: entrepreneurship is a vital and rewarding calling for anyone who wishes to start his or her own business. Entrepreneurship brings the promise of joy and riches few others will ever enjoy, working as they do in somebody else's business—the *job* as it's called. The job is the place where the life is taken out of us one day at a time, where our hearts become deadened, where the thrill of new ideas is most often met with a deaf ear, where creativity is most often nonexistent, and where passion is reduced to the thrill of knowing the weekend is just around the corner. Thank God for the weekend! What a limited world!

In this book, Loral gives you a stunning option: any one of you can make the leap to becoming joyfully and fruitfully independent in a business of your own. Loral walks with you every step of the way, a passionate, evocative, intelligent, and committed guide who knows even before you take the first step exactly where your foot will falter, and what to do when it does, so that you may never fear getting lost.

So, settle down. Read slowly. Savor each step. Loral is here!

To you and yours, good reading. And better yet, have a wonderful journey together. Your life will never be the same.

Michael E. Gerber
Carlsbad, California
author of *The E-Myth Revisited*

Acknowledgments

A big advantage to building Cash Machines is the number of terrific people who come into your life. Teams have helped me create many businesses, and those businesses continue to generate my dream teams. I am very fortunate to have so many great people involved in my Wealth Cycle and my life. I thank you all, and I'd like to name a few.

First, my main teammate in life, Carl Logrecco. Thank you for all we create together.

Thank you to the McGraw-Hill crew, especially Jeanne Glasser, Lynda Luppino, Philip Ruppel, Keith Fox, and Lydia Rinaldi. Thank you also to Ruth Mannino and your eagle-eyed crew. Huge thanks to Caroline Sherman for the amazing work. Thank you also to Melanie, Stacey, Wendy and Suzanne for getting the word out, and many thanks to the Premier team for our joint venture.

Big thanks to Fred Auzennne, Wendy and Gary Byford, Irene Erklidis, Martha Hanlon, David Mleczko, Steve Parker, Jay Pearson,

James Sheppard, Sue Walker, Chris Williams, and David Zebny for your thoughts on Cash Machines. You all know how to build excitement, as well as businesses, and I appreciate your keeping it fun. And thanks again, of course, to Mark Meyerdirk.

The Live Out Loud Cash Machine continues to fuel my Wealth Cycle with excellent skills, brave ideas, and first-rate execution. Thank you to the strategists, coaches, and Field Partners who support the visions and values of so many. Continued appreciation and thanks to the Live Out Loud team, especially Tina, Karin, Irene, Holly, Sandi, Amy, and Rebekah, who make sure our 120-day plans happen no matter what.

I'm consistently energized by the personalities at our Big Tables, and I thank you all for pursuing your goals so tirelessly. It's inspiring. Each session, as we make more and more millionaires, I'm constantly affirmed.

The farm was the first Cash Machine I ever toiled on, and so thank you to my parents, my sister Holly, and my brothers, Jeff, Doug, and Kent, for helping me learn early on that good people make good business. And as always, thank you Aunt Bev, for assuring me that I already had the skills to go for it.

The Wealth Cycle is all about building a bigger and better life. Logan, Tristin, and Carl give me that better life every day. Thank you to the family machine, the best team I've got.

LORAL LANGEMEIER

THE
MILLIONAIRE MAKER'S GUIDE
TO
CREATING A CASH MACHINE FOR LIFE

Introduction

Driving down the main street of my town, a great little resort town in a mountainous area of the Northwest, I pass several retail stores, some restaurants, beauty and wellness salons, office buildings, and shingles hung by various professionals. Commercials blare from the radio. And the people in the cars around me are on their way to make or use some product or service.

Entrepreneurship surrounds us. New businesses and ventures are the very pulse of wealth around the world. The fact is, almost every product or service that we use, each storefront or office building that you pass, is a symbol of bravery. Some individual had to have the courage and faith to create that product or build that business. If not for the vision, skills, energy, effort, and, most important, persistence of an entreprenuer, that product or service, store, or company would not exist.

I'm pretty sure that Christopher Columbus did not cross the ocean so that we could all get jobs and secure our 401(k)s. Entrepreneurship *is* America. If it hadn't been for Henry Ford, you would not be driving that car. If it hadn't been for Sam Walton, you'd have no Wal-Mart to frequent. And if it hadn't been for Clarence Birdseye, the only thing you'd be pulling out of the freezer would be ice. The results of these entrepreneurs' efforts are ingrained in our life, yet we mostly take their products and services for granted. I know I didn't offer thanks to Margaret Rudkin every time I bit into a Pepperidge Farm cookie while writing this book—though I should have. In my pregnant state, that was quite often, thank you very much.

Entrepreneurship is the single biggest source of wealth in this country. Yet too many wealth-building programs bypass this step. This book is about building and sustaining a viable business to help you create and support your wealth. That business is called a Cash Machine.

Defined, a Cash Machine is a *legitimate, legally structured business venture* that uses your *skill sets,* is *modeled* after a similar successful business, is developed in *weeks,* sometimes days, takes advantage of *teamwork,* and generates *immediate cash* to feed your Wealth Cycle. The Wealth Cycle is my proprietary system for wealth building, which I wrote about in my first two McGraw-Hill books, *The Millionaire Maker* and *The Millionaire Maker's Guide to Wealth Cycle Investing.* The Wealth Cycle is just that: a cycle of wealth. It is a systematic approach to building assets that generate passive income. That passive income is then used to invest in more assets. The Cash Machine is a key part of that wonderful cycle of assets and income. Creating businesses and making investments, not managing expenses or focusing on debt, is the way to get wealthy. That may seem too obvious to be a big "aha" moment, yet for some reason most people, and far too many personal finance programs, spend too much time focused on controlling debt. That makes your life small, and I'm not interested in making your life small. I'm all about creating a healthy, fun, want-to life. Forget about a savings plan, and consider instead the excitement of a spending plan. Let go of retirement restrictions, and strive for a Freedom Day. Stop planning for poverty, and start a plan for prosperity. I don't know about you, but as I get older I don't want my life to shrink; I want it to expand. The Cash Machine is your link to this expansion.

If you want to sit around counting pennies and live a smaller, have-to life, then focus on your debt. In fact, I promise you that if you spend the next year focused on getting your debt down to nothing, you will have exactly that at the end of the year—nothing. Focusing on debt is like dieting without exercise. It's an endless cycle of starvation and deprivation with no lasting results. However, if you spend this next year building a business, you will break every unproductive financial cycle you've ever had.

The Wealth Cycle and the Cash Machine are all about expansion, living larger, and finding a bigger, better life. You do not have to sacrifice your lust for latte to become wealthy. A colleague of mine drinks three iced quad venti nonfat no-whip mochas a day. His monthly coffee habit is some people's car payment. Yet by using the Wealth Cycle, creating a Cash Machine, and directly investing in assets, his net worth has gone from half a million dollars to four million dollars in just three years. Wealth building should be about excitement, not sacrifice. Let's face it: *you cannot save your way to double-digit growth.*

This building rather than shrinking is the secret of the Cash Machine, and it's the way to wealth. The Cash Machine allows you to add to your life. Building a business as an asset is one of the most powerful forms of wealth generation and one of the best steps you can take to create an expansive, empowering life.

I bet you've had a good idea for a business, but I'll also guess that:

1. You think new product development is best left to the inventor in his garage.
2. You think starting up a new business takes too much time, money, and energy.

3. You don't want to leave the safe confines of your job.
4. You've tried to start a business before and had little luck.
5. You already have a business, and it's taking up too much of your time, creating lots of stress for you and, the real kicker, not making any more money than you did on your W-2.

From what I've seen, many who do pursue their dream quit quickly, never make any money, and learn nothing about how to run a business. That is not fun. The Cash Machine is different. In this approach to entrepreneurship you make money immediately, learn increasingly advanced business skills, and ultimately build and generate wealth and your dream life.

Traditional teaching of entrepreneurship suggests that you begin with an idea. Not here. We begin with what you already know so that you can get going and make money immediately. The best part is, you do not have to go it alone. A key component of the Cash Machine is *team*. This book is for those of you who want to partner with others who have a team or create your own team to

1. Build a new business.
2. Fix an existing business.
3. Buy a business.

The Cash Machine may or may not be your dream business. And it is definitely not a business venture that oversees your investments, your assets, or your passive income. It is a separate entity, a moneymaking machine derived from skills you already have that will allow you to set up shop as soon as possible. You may not realize it, but you already have the skills, intelligence, and energy to build something valuable. The only thing you don't have is the way, the right way, to make a lot of money from what you already know. The Cash Machine will help you do just that. The good news is that it's never too late to start. With a Cash Machine, you will *learn to earn* and *make money*—fast.

Entrepreneurs are the backbone of the capitalist system. In this country alone, thousands of small businesses are created every day. The problem is that too many budding entrepreneurs have no idea what they're doing. These businesses are rarely profitable, and eventually, most fizzle and die. With a Cash Machine, you *learn* to earn. The only real way to learn how to run a business is by running a business. You've got to do it. And, let's face it, learning is not its own reward. It is no fun to learn if you're not making money. Theory is nice, but a little reward goes a long way in keeping anyone motivated. With the Cash Machine approach to entrepreneurship, you learn to earn and you make more money immediately.

Your Cash Machine and your investments in assets are the 50–50 partnership that creates and accelerates your Wealth Cycle. The cash flow from your Cash Machine seeds your assets and fuels the Wealth Cycle. In order to be wealthy, you need a Cash Machine.

In addition to being the fuel for generating wealth, the Cash Machine is a gateway to unleashing your vision. Without your vision, skills, energy, effort, and, most important, persistence, some product or service, store, or company will not exist. Innovation is at the heart of this great country, and if you pursue your wealth by creating a business, then you too will contribute to the fabric and future of our nation. Let's begin one of the most exciting ventures on your wealth-building journey—the Cash Machine.

CHAPTER ONE

The Cash Machine

Making More Money as You Learn to Earn

A permission-based society is exhausting. I knew a woman, Marilyn Stanley, who was energetic, fun, and smart—when she wasn't working. While she was working, Marilyn was frustrated and bored. Yet she was committed to the commute. She indentured herself to work 10 hours a day, 5 days a week, 50 weeks a year so that she could continue to spend most of her time being frustrated and bored. I don't get that. Marilyn and I talked about what she could do.

"I have to work that much," she said. "I have an adult life; I have responsibilities." That mentality will keep anyone in debt. I've met too many people who used to play like rock stars, then became responsible for families and started making decisions out of fear that they'd risk their security. In other words, they played not to lose. That is not how you win. You can't be afraid to lose—you have to be committed to winning.

Marilyn was working 50 hours a week as a graphic designer at an Internet provider and barely broke even after taxes. But she felt lucky to have a job. Marilyn needed the money to help support her family and pay off her debts. She felt trapped, but she was worried about rocking the boat. She was eager to find a way to make more money without putting her livelihood at risk. Marilyn dreamed of a way to ensure and expand her financial future on her own terms.

Then there was Al Cypress. Al was in business for himself and had a pretty good venture. He was a sports psychologist, and he had set up shop in a strip mall in Los Angeles. He had a few dozen regular clients and several drop-ins every month. Al was proud of his business and his ability to get it off the ground, but he discovered that he was working more hours and making even less money than he did when he worked as the in-house therapist for a large corporation. He felt that he was pursuing his vision, yet his business was draining all of his time and energy. He wondered how he could possibly continue this way.

Another woman I coached, Rosa Brackett, had some assets, including equity in her home, investments in the stock market, and an IRA. A widow, she feared that she would forever be at the mercy of a fixed income, limited to a world that would get smaller as she got older. Rosa had always wanted to build a nonprofit company that would give underprivileged children access to crafts and artisan workshops. However, she had no idea how to run a business, let alone start such an organization. Rosa knew that it was time for her to dust off her dreams and take control of her life and her future.

At first glance, these three people may seem to have nothing in common. But the fact is that each of them could, and did, benefit from a Cash Machine. Regardless of whether you find yourself barely making ends meet in a W-2 job, running a business that's more aggravating than rewarding, or holding on to lazy assets that narrow your choices for the future, a Cash Machine will help you make more money, learn to earn, and get control of your life.

The Cash Machine begins with the answer to this question: "What are your skills?" These skills, the things you already know how to do and are comfortable doing, are the kernel of a profitable Cash Machine. You will derive the idea for a business from the answer to that question. This won't be just any idea; it will be your *fastest path to cash*. Within weeks of building, fixing, or buying a Cash Machine, you will make more money.

This model of entrepreneurship, the Cash Machine, was developed from my personal experience in creating new businesses. I started my first business when I was 17, and since then, I have built a number of businesses in a variety of industries, several of which have grossed millions. Most of the wealth builders I work with in the Live Out Loud community own businesses or are getting ones started. This is a fundamental part of the Wealth Cycle.

The Wealth Cycle is built on 12 building blocks, all of which work together to generate cash flow to build wealth and maintain that wealth. These are explained in full in *The Millionaire Maker* book. Three of the building blocks—Financial Baseline, Freedom Day, and Gap Analysis—are tools for uncovering where you are and where you need to go. Three others—leadership, teamwork, and conditioning—are action steps that are necessary to support the process. Four of the building blocks—entities, forecasting, Wealth Accounts, and debt management—are core strategies that ensure moneymaking and wealth building. And two of the building blocks—directly allocated investments (i.e., assets) and an entrepreneurial venture (i.e., a Cash Machine)—are the essential tactics to make more money. My last book, *The Millionaire Maker's Guide to Wealth Cycle Investing*, focused on assets. This book is about the Cash Machine. Let's look at the different ways you can approach the Cash Machine.

Build It, Fix It, Buy It

Build It

Starting from scratch, with little money and no other assets, is not the easiest way to begin a business, but the Cash Machine makes it much less difficult. By using *the skills you have* to build a business, you can start making money fast. You can also *partner* with someone who is starting a company from scratch in order to leverage your skills with their ideas. I've brought in Cash Machine partners to run a few of my businesses, and it worked out very well. I benefited from their skills and knowledge and got my ideas executed. They benefited from my team and vision and had a chance to make money with, as well as manage, an entrepreneurial venture.

Some advantages of building a company are that you usually have

- No hidden problems
- Control over the business's direction
- The option to tailor the venture to your lifestyle

Some disadvantages of building a company are that you have

- No name recognition
- No customers
- No instant cash flow
- An unproven entity

The decision to build a business has to be made from experience, not emotion. Because we are looking for immediate, money-making ventures, you want to choose a start-up venture that is easily accessible and achievable. Big ideas wrapped up in emotion usually are not simple. We want simple. The big ideas come later in wealth building. For now, you want to do what's already been done by others so that you can learn how to do it too. The Marilyn Stanley case study explored over the course of the following chapters provides a good example of the *build it* approach.

Fix It

If you have your own business, but it's not making enough money or it's too difficult to run, then you do not have an effective Cash Machine. Too many people pursue a business without making any money. That's not a business, that's a hobby. Hobbies do not make you wealthy. If you have a business that is broken, or if you are partnering in a broken business, then you must shift to a new way of thinking about that business in order to turn it into a Cash Machine. The result will be a venture that makes money and has the potential to grow into a long-term asset with multiple streams of income. Throughout this book, we will follow Al Cypress's Cash Machine as an example of *fix it.*

Buy It

If you have assets in the form of home equity, CDs, money market accounts, and so on, you might consider turning those lazy assets into assets that generate greater returns. You can do this by liquidating them and using the cash to buy a business that is capable of creating cash flow. If you don't have assets or any money, but you like the idea of buying an ongoing Cash Machine, you can join another entrepreneur or a group of investors that are buying a company and offer your skills and experience as *sweat equity.*

There are hundreds of different types of businesses for sale all the time. Although owning a car wash or a Laundromat may not appeal to you, acquiring such a business can be a very efficient learning tool, as can buying into well-researched and reputable franchises and multilevel-marketing companies. When buying a Cash Machine it is important to consider your lifestyle expectations. If you can't handle early mornings or powdered sugar on your hands, then a doughnut shop would not be a good acquisition. Although you may have hired a great doughnut maker, inevitably he or she will call in sick, and it will be you watching the dough rise with the sun.

Some advantages of buying an existing business are

- Immediate cash flow
- Accelerated learning curve
- Reduction in start-up cost
- Preexisting customers
- Easier financing

Some disadvantages of buying an existing business are

- Initial purchase price
- Possible hidden problems, such as
  - Uncollected receivables
  - Existing employee issues
  - Equipment needs

Another option for buying a business is to consider a franchise. Some advantages of franchises include

- Brand identity
- Training program
- Existing marketing plan
- Proven business model
- Financing options

Some disadvantages of buying a franchise include

- High cost of entry
- Limited flexibility
- Potential cap on growth
- Reliance on the franchiser's supply chain, designs, and the like
- Franchise royalty and ad fees
- An operating agreement written for the franchiser's benefit

When you buy a business, whether it is a traditional company or a franchise, you must perform *due diligence,* which means that you have to research the opportunity extensively. This is the only way to manage *risk.* As with any investment, there are risks to be assessed when buying a Cash Machine. These include product risks, industry risks, and economic risks. Educating yourself about any opportunity can help you minimize risk, and conducting due diligence will help you assess the possible pitfalls and problems.

In addition to investigating the wide range of possible strengths and weaknesses, opportunities and threats of the potential purchase, finding a profitable company at the right price can be difficult. As with many things, sellers and owners often have an inflated perception of a business's value, and potential buyers are responsible for uncovering hidden costs and hurdles to cash flow. The process of due diligence—that is, research and investigation—is essential when buying a company. If buying a Cash Machine is the route you choose to take, then you will need the help of a CPA, an attorney, and possibly a financial coach who can help with due diligence. I also suggest that you join the professional associations relevant to the sector in which your business competes. Their trade magazines and Web sites will give you much needed information, as well as multiples and metrics to use for valuation. Due diligence will make or break your decision. If you do not have the capacity to carry out due diligence, then you are not ready to own and operate a business. The example of Rosa Brackett's Cash Machine will take us through an experience of how to *buy it.*

A note on straddling: you can create a Cash Machine while you still have your commitment to a 9 to 5 job. This is *straddling,* and most of the wealth builders with whom I work take this approach. A Cash Machine is not a license to tear up the punch card but rather an avenue to get into entrepreneurship quickly and easily. When you first create your Cash Machine, you'll straddle the fence between where you were and where you're going. In less time than you think, you will be successful enough in your business to leave your job and move on to a bigger and better business. It usually takes this *straddling* time to learn that your skills are in fact worth a lot more money than the average W-2 employer is willing to fork over. You've probably realized by now that *you do not get paid what you're worth; you get paid what you negotiate.* You can negotiate a lot better when you're in charge.

Though initially it may be necessary for you to straddle, it is not easy. I did this for several months, working for a large corporation whiile trying to get what eventually became Live Out Loud off the ground. Just as I did, many straddlers want to have secure benefits before taking the leap. Others are reluctant to make a mistake. It took me a while to decide that I just needed to make the leap and figure it all out later.

Though straddling is a necessary step for most W-2 earners, the common problem for straddlers is not having enough time to do both the W-2 job and the Cash Machine. You need to continue to do your job and do it right, or you're not being fair to your current employer. If you don't have enough time, you need a team. And since no one has enough time, everyone needs a team. By building Cash Machine teams to help them do the work and cultivate sales, straddlers can shift the balance away from the W-2 job and toward the Cash Machine until they can finally focus on their business full time. Eventually, this has to happen. If you never jump ship, your business is just a hobby. You can't put enough time into a hobby to make it grow, and a Cash Machine must grow.

A note on partnering: partnering can work in many ways. One is that you take your idea and combine it with another person's. This works best if the ideas and the people are complementary. It also works if people with two complementary skill sets want to buy and/or fix an existing business together. I've seen all sorts of combinations, many of which have worked with great success. I've seen a teacher partner with a techie and an actor to create educational videos. I've seen a factory supervisor join forces with an art gallery manager to buy a housewares manufacturer. I've seen a salon professional reach out to a doctor to help improve his business by bringing in a wellness program. The partnership possibilities are endless. In fact, I'm an investor in a home décor company that was launched by an artist and a business professional who combined their skill sets.

Another approach is to bring your business idea to an existing business. Ideas are a dime a dozen, and *execution is everything.* That's why the consumer warehouse retailer might pay the sock manufacturer just a buck a pair while taking four dollars itself. But, believe it or not, I think that's fair. It takes one hot shower to get a good product idea into your head. Getting the product into the hands of consumers takes a lot more effort. New product ideas may work best with an existing infrastructure and through an established channel of distribution. Huge success stories have come out of these types of arrangements and can be beneficial to everyone involved.

Another approach to partnering does not require you to have an idea at all. This partnership relies on your skills. By taking your skill set into a business, you are providing a valued service to the start-up. I knew a woman with extensive brand and consumer product packaging experience who wanted to get in on a start-up operation. She had no ideas for her own Cash Machine, nor did she have a desire, necessarily, to build something from an idea of her own or buy a company. She had embarked on her Wealth Cycle, though, and a Cash Machine was necessary. Recent work events gave her the luxury of not having to make too much money right away or to hang on to her old job. And so she took an executive job with a brand new company, at a fair salary and with the promise of a percentage of ownership, that is, sweat equity.

Partnering is a very efficient approach to the Cash Machine for wealth builders who do not want to run their own business just yet. This "work-with-it" alternative allows you to learn to earn on someone else's skill set. The glitch, sometimes, is that you might not make more money, at least not initially. If you have the time and resources to take a low-paying or no-paying job with a start-up company, this is another path to getting entrepreneurship skills under your belt. It requires finding a well-run start-up company managed by a smart entrepreneurial team from which you can learn these skills.

There's also *short-term to learn* partnering. Many of those who build, fix, or buy a Cash Machine can benefit from *shadowing* a business owner during the business modeling stage, if only for a day. I once worked for a bookkeeping company for 4 months, 13 hours a week, at $17 an hour, just to see how the company was run and to learn a new skill set. It was not my most favorite thing to do, but a mentor had suggested it, and as a result, I got the knowledge and the team I needed. Experience is much more effective than a lecture or a workbook, and getting in and getting it done is the best learning tool there is.

Keeping It Real

Whether you build, fix, or buy your Cash Machine (and many wealth builders have done all three at some time in their lives), you are going to focus on a business that generates revenue immediately. This business is not built on a dream or a clever idea. It's a sure thing.

Eventually, once you have the ability and knowledge to run and build a company, you can create a Cash Machine to serve your vision.

The Cash Machine keeps it simple and realistic. We focus on the fundamentals of entrepreneurship and the objective of making more money right now. If you haven't tried to make more money outside of your job, we're going to find a business idea for you by discovering your fastest path to cash. If you already have a business, but it's just not doing much for your wealth, we'll focus on making it a moneymaker.

The approach to creating a Cash Machine is straightforward. We look at your current situation and your objectives, consider your skill set and abilities, and then create a plan that optimizes both the situation and your skills. As you'll see, we get off and running right away.

CASH MACHINE ACTION PLAN

Discover the skills you already have.

Generate a business idea based on those skills.

Model the idea after a similar business.

Test the sales potential through revenue modeling.

Design a Cash Machine plan.

Build a team.

Develop the marketing and sales strategies.

The way we begin the process is a distinction of the Cash Machine. Most entrepreneurs begin with the idea, but because the requirement for a Cash Machine is that it be up and running immediately, you need an edge. That edge is the skills you already have.

Whether you know it or not, you have many skills at your disposal that could make you money tomorrow. You may like these skills and find them fun—for example, you're great with kids, and you enjoy being with kids. Or you may not like these skills—for example, you're good at fixing things, but you don't enjoy it. The issue is not whether or not you enjoy doing something; the issue is whether you can immediately make money doing it.

Unlike those who say, "Do what you love. The money will follow," I live in the world of reality. You might love to paint, but selling your originals on the sidewalk is a tough gig. On the other hand, if you like making pies, you know there's demand for them at your local flea market, and you can make money doing this tomorrow; then you get to do what you like in your Cash Machine right now. Eventually, the painter will get to sell paintings, and they may become part of a Cash Machine down the road, but for now, the painter must learn how to build a business that will bring in cash immediately. Believe me, when the money starts coming in fast, you'll begin to love what you do. Start with what you know how to do, and you will get to do what you love later on.

With a Cash Machine, you

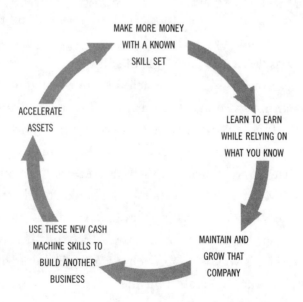

Then go around again. Those are the life stages of your Cash Machine.

If you start this process today, you'll find that you're going to have more money coming in faster, you'll retain more of that money through proper *entity structuring* and *forecasting strategies,* and you'll be on your way to being your own boss in a world you've created in less time than you ever thought possible. The Cash Machine gets you past "ready-set" and right to "go" in a way that no theoretical MBA approach ever could. In fact, I work with a lot of MBAs who say that they never learned the practical, day-to-day, business-building skills that we teach here.

The First 24 Hours in a Cash Machine

Marilyn Stanley realized that she would benefit from having a Cash Machine. Her known skill set was graphic design, and she had some organizational and time management skills as well. She and her husband were both 40, with two kids, and had no real money invested for the future. Marilyn was finding her job tedious and not financially rewarding. She needed to make more money. And that meant creating a Cash Machine.

Al Cypress was a good example of someone who already had his own business, but was not approaching it in a way that would lead to great wealth. As you may have realized if you already own a business, it's no fun to replace your W-2 job with a burdensome 24-hours-a-day entrepreneurial venture. Maybe that allows you to say, "Well, at least I'm working for myself." But even when you have your own company, you still have others—the bank, your investors, your customers or clients, your suppliers and vendors—to whom you have to answer. Being your own boss is nice, but it can also be a nightmare. That's why we approach a Cash Machine with specific objectives. We want to create a business that

1. Is profitable
2. You can eventually build into or convert into something you enjoy
3. Doesn't take over your life forever

4. Generates wealth
5. Serves your vision

Al Cypress needed his company to help him create a great future for himself, not exhaust him. He needed to fix the business and make it a Cash Machine.

Rosa Brackett was simply not leading the life she wanted. She needed to take the assets she had, investment decisions made by her late husband, and restructure them to better serve her vision for the crafts and artisan workshops. She could do this by buying a Cash Machine.

Marilyn, Al, and Rosa all pursued a Cash Machine to improve their lives and reach their goals. Though these are not their real names, these case studies, and all of the case studies in this book, represent real clients who are now on their way to great wealth through a Cash Machine.

Let's look at how Marilyn came to discover her own Cash Machine. It began with the *Gap Analysis.* Defined, the Gap Analysis is the Wealth Cycle approach to mapping out a plan to get from where you are to where you want to be. The Gap Analysis is derived from the wealth builder's answers to the following eight questions.

CASH MACHINE CASE IN POINT

From Skill Set to Start-Up

Marilyn Stanley and her husband both had full-time jobs, she at an Internet service provider, he as a building maintenance supervisor. They had two kids and lived in Palo Alto, California.

1. What is your monthly pretax income?
   "I make $43,000 a year, and my husband makes about $50,000," she said. "That's $3,583 a month pretax from me and $4,167 from him, so $7,750." *(continues)*

(continued)

2. What are your monthly expenditures?

"We are a family of four living in Palo Alto. We are lucky if we spend less than $5,000 a month. The kids are in private school, so that's a lot of money right there."

3. What are your assets?

"Our home is worth about $600,000, and we have $100,000 of equity in it. We have retirement plans, maybe $50,000, and we have about $25,000 in stock in my company."

4. What are your liabilities?

"We have a $500,000 mortgage and credit card debt of maybe $8,000."

5. What else?

"You mean what have I forgotten? Well, I think my son has some coins in his closet. But besides that, no, we don't have any hidden IRAs or anything like that."

6. What do you want?

"We'd like to see our kids through college, pay off this house, and I think we'd both like to quit our jobs sooner rather than later. We'd like to just travel and have fun."

7. What are the skills you use to make money?

"My skills are *graphic design, technology,* and *Web languages;* I'm comfortable with the Web. I'm *organized,* and I *manage my time* at work so that I can get home. I'm the *chauffeur* for all my kids' activities—is that a skill set, driving? My husband is a maintenance supervisor, so he has a lot of *mechanical* and *electrical* skills, and he knows about *machinery* and *building stuff.* He also has a *wood shop* in the basement."

8. Are you willing to create and execute a Wealth Cycle?

She knew the only answer to this: "Yes."

Marilyn's answers to these questions made it very clear that this family did not have enough money to live without financial frustration, let alone live well. Let's look at how Marilyn went from where she was to building a Cash Machine.

In my Cash Machine seminars, we create Cash Machine Makeovers.

CASH MACHINE MAKEOVER

FREEDOM PLAN

What I want financially per year from my Cash Machine _____

Ideas for my Cash Machine _____

Revenue to be generated _____

BUSINESS MODEL	SALES IDEAS	MARKETING IDEAS	TEAM

BASELINE

Current skills and how I get paid now _____

How much money I make _____

The most amount of money I have ever made _____

Let's look at how Marilyn went from where she was to building a Cash Machine. The action plan, seven weeks to sales, also serves as an outline for this book. In the following chapters, we'll cover each of these topics in more detail. The number of weeks listed here is not hard and fast. You can do all of these things in 24 hours. I've seen it. If you have the resources and the energy to plow ahead, do them as soon as you can. There's leeway to do as much as soon as possible, but you can't exceed seven weeks. None of the tasks can be held over. Ideas must be generated by week 2, and while you should be building your team all along, most of the initial positions should be filled, at least on paper, by week 6.

Action Plan: Seven Weeks to Sales

Action Plan						
Seven Weeks to Sales						
Week 1	Week 2	Week 3	Week 4	Week 5	Week 6	Week 7
Skills	Idea	Business Model	Revenue Model	Cash Machine Plan	Team	Marketing and Sales

Discover Your *Skills*

Skill sets are the seed of the Cash Machine, so we began with Marilyn's answer to the seventh question. Her answers revealed that her skill set included graphic and Web site design, technology, communication, organization, and management. And Marilyn was right; driving is a skill that can make money. I've seen many a Cash Machine begin with airport limousine and errand pickup services.

Generate the *Idea*

Starting with her skill set, Marilyn brainstormed with her husband, friends, and colleagues about business ideas. She also asked her kids for advice. Children should be included in all aspects of the Cash Machine. It's similar to immersing them in a second language. They will get fluent in a healthy financial consciousness, which will shape their money decisions and conditioning for the rest of their lives. The idea that surfaced from Marilyn's brainstorming sessions was a Web site design company.

Model Your Idea

Creating a Web site design company was not an original idea. And that was a good thing. Marilyn needed to find a similar business with a successful operation upon which she could model her own. Someone is always already playing a bigger, better game, and reinventing the wheel is a slow process. She would then need to build on these models with a *unique selling proposition* to make her business distinct, and thus more marketable.

Talking to mentors in the same field or shadowing business owners is an efficient learning tool. As soon as you decide on an idea, you must find out how it's already been done. Imitation is not only the sincerest form of flattery; it's the simplest route to profitability. A quick Internet search will get you to many business models, and the answers to your questions will be a phone call or visit away. As long as you don't set yourself up as a competitor (don't call the local scrapbook expert and tell her that you want to start the same business next door), you'll be pleasantly surprised by how eager others are to share their advice. It's best to call someone in a faraway market who could potentially become a mentor or a strategic partner. Conversely, someone in the local market might be interested in helping you if your efforts can somehow help that person expand his client base. Strategic partnerships are usually most successful with a complementary business and not an identical model, but anything is possible.

Revenue Model

Based on what she discovered from looking at similar businesses and talking to those running them, Marilyn calculated a *Revenue Model*. In this short and sweet analysis, Marilyn decided

- How much money she wanted to make. In a Cash Machine, business owners do not declare what they think they *can* make; they state what they *will* make and then create a Cash Machine that supports that goal.

In order to make that target number, Marilyn then calculated

- How much she would charge
- How many clients she would need
- How many hours she would need to work
- The expenses associated with the revenues

The revenue model helps you decide if it's feasible to charge the prices required *and* get the number of customers or clients necessary *and* put in the hours that will make the amount of money targeted. If the numbers are doable—that is, if you can work the hours, charge those prices, get those clients or customers, and do so profitably—then you are all set to move forward. If not, it's back to the idea stage.

One of the best things about the Cash Machine is that it's built on the idea of a team. If a ballerina decides to teach dance, but she can't reach her target revenue number because of the number of hours required, she can hire other dancers and scale out the model. In Marilyn's case, she felt that even with her full-time job and family responsibilities, she could work the number of hours she'd calculated and make the amount of money she desired. It was on to the next stage.

Design the *Cash Machine Plan*

Marilyn drafted a very concise plan that helped her to better flesh out the idea. This involved looking at

- The concept
- The opportunity to sell her concept in the marketplace
- A strategy to market the product

- How the business itself would be organized with regard to her
    - Team
    - Operations, including systems and entity structuring
    - Financials, including projections

Not only does the Cash Machine Plan give you some guidance and direction, but it can also be used to attract the attention of potential investors and strategic partners. You'll find that the growth of your Cash Machine requires constant conversation, and the plan is a good reference for those conversations.

Build Your *Team*

Once Marilyn had a general idea of her business concept and knew that it would be financially viable, she needed to surround herself with a team that would help make the business work. Team building begins on day 1 and is a constant part of the Cash Machine. In Marilyn's case, she'd already begun to do this in the brainstorming stage. Marilyn needed to find and *legally contract* with her employees, suppliers, and any partners she'd need. She also needed support players, such as an accountant, bookkeeper, and legal counsel. Additionally, *life support* is often necessary for the Cash Machine owner. I have a great support group—Team Langemeier—that helps with my home and family. When I was pregnant, my brain was very busy making another brain; I really needed a team. You too will find that it's worth it to pay a housekeeper $10 or $20 an hour for four hours a week so that you can focus on making thousands of dollars an hour. The last time I checked, most millionaires don't do their own laundry.

Despite myths to the contrary, there have never been entrepreneurs who are Lone Rangers. Successful wealth builders do not go out into the business world alone. It just doesn't happen. The best leaders gather support around them so that they can do more with less of their own time and energy. The goal of the Cash Machine is to grow, not to set up shop on the corner and bring in a few bucks every week. A Cash Machine is about building a big, wealth-generating business, and that takes a team.

Develop the *Marketing and Sales* Strategies

Now that she had the foundation in place, Marilyn was ready to start the business. The ramp-up to any business is marketing and sales. She needed to get the word out to her potential customers. In the Cash Machine, this is done initially with guerrilla marketing, such as flyers and e-mail blasts or other creative tactics, such as informal, Tupperware party–type gatherings. Eventually, these efforts build into a more enduring marketing strategy that supports the Cash Machine as it matures.

The Entrepreneurial Skill Set

As soon as the business is up and running and revenue starts coming in the door, the Cash Machine owner is ready to move on to learning and understanding new skills, the entrepreneurial skill set. These are the skills it takes to run not just this business, but any business. This is yet another way in which the Cash Machine is different from traditional approaches to teaching entrepreneurship. In the classic model, you learn, and then you do. Here, you will start your business, make money, and then learn what the heck it is you are doing. Sure, it's exciting, but if you work off of skills you know and surround yourself with experience, and by that I mean a team, you minimize your risk.

Marilyn now needed to take on, and come to understand, some other skills:

Entrepreneurial Skill Set				
Management	Marketing	Sales	Operations	Finance

Management

There's no getting around the fact that a business takes vision and vision takes *leadership*. In addition to her apparent skill set, Marilyn needed to look at the management skills she'd need, as well as her psychology and conditioning, to get all of her ducks in a row.

Marketing

Too many businesses spend time attracting their initial customers and then stop their marketing efforts. Marketing is continuous and encompasses much more than advertising or signage. It begins at the idea stage, constructing a concept that meets the needs of the marketplace, and should be carried all the way through every step of the business life cycle. Marilyn learned how to market her Web design service continuously, and this kept her product in demand and her pipeline of projects full.

Sales

Too many people fear selling. And that's because they go about it the wrong way. The key to effective sales is enrollment. Successful companies tap into a need with a positive experience. Marilyn was good at marketing, but she was nervous about the final sale, or "the close." Marketing gets customers to the door. Sales makes them want to take their coats off and stay awhile. Pursuing one and not the other is useless. Marilyn had to become good at sales.

Operations

Marilyn needed to establish the operations for her business. Systems, such as accounting, customer databases, marketing, tech support, and sales, would all find a place in her Cash Machine. Additionally, she needed to structure a legal entity to protect the business and help maximize constructive tax strategies. Gathering and leading the personnel necessary to help her manage these structures and systems, as well as get her product out the door, would also be part of this skill set.

Finance

The Cash Machine required Marilyn to become more comfortable with numbers. It started with

- Revenue modeling

and continued on through

- Profits and losses—the income statement
- Assets and liabilities—the balance sheet
- Sources and uses of cash—the cash flow statement

Marilyn had to become very familiar with the quantitative side of any business. Every Cash Machine owner gets to know these statements intimately. It's not as daunting as you might think, and running numbers soon becomes as easy as flipping channels. Well, okay, not quite as easy. But it's definitely more satisfying and productive.

The ability to look at numbers and see a bigger picture or make an important decision based on a small detail in the numbers is useful in any and every business. It's also helpful in every aspect of wealth building, and the Cash Machine is a quick and effective way to learn these skills.

Accelerating Assets

Every day people create businesses that might look like Cash Machines, but are not. The difference is that a Cash Machine is not about bringing home a bit of extra money with a little business. I've seen people create a Revenue Model with $100,000 a year as their target and think that's a home run. That's not even a single. Having a Cash Machine doesn't mean having a small corner drugstore where you lose money but give away lollipops. A Cash Machine is about learning to build a business that generates lots of wealth for you and your family for generations to come. If you set yourself up to sell scarves at the local fair, but you have not created a Revenue Model, set up an entity, developed a bigger marketing plan, or built a team, you have not created a Cash Machine.

Once your business is up and running, which should happen in months, if not weeks or even days, it's time to accelerate the business and really build it. With her business up and running, Marilyn considered creating ancillary products and services. She also looked at branching out into other businesses altogether by investing her time and money in several related and nonrelated business ventures and assets.

You get into your Cash Machine with a plan for its future. This includes *exit strategies*. There are several different options for realizing wealth from the business asset you've created. Although your Cash Machine may work as an ongoing venture and provide you with an endless annuity, you might also want to sell the asset as a private or public venture, or consider other liquidation choices.

These are the elements of the Cash Machine. Obviously, some take more time than others. For instance, marketing and sales should take about 60 percent of your energy. In the meantime, managing your debt as part of your finances should take some time to set up, but should occupy less than 1 percent of your time after that.

Nothing I teach is that difficult. It's just different. In fact, I've found that the idea of a Cash Machine is so simple and straightforward that some people think they already understand it and delve right in, as they should, and maybe skip a step or two, which they shouldn't.

Sequencing your Cash Machine, which means doing the right thing at the right time, is vital. Mistakes occur when wealth builders hop right into one part of the process without considering and executing each step. This happens a lot because, sometimes, starting a business can seem like child's play.

CASH MACHINE CASE IN POINT

The Lemonade Stand

Fifth graders Sam and Sally needed $100 by the end of the week. Natural wealth builders, they had a chance to invest in a treehouse share that one of their clever little friends was starting. Not only did they want to invest, but they wanted to learn something about business so that they could do something similar to their friend's business one day. Their objective was to make more money and learn to earn. They decided that a lemonade stand was their fastest path to cash. They'd seen some friends do one last weekend, and they thought they could model the way those people did it. They also did some revenue modeling. They knew that they wanted to walk away with $100 after covering their expenses of $10, and so their goal was $110. They figured they'd charge 50 cents a glass, and they aimed to sell 220 glasses by the end of the day.

Early on a Saturday morning, they coaxed their parents into lending them $10 to buy the lemons, sugar, ice, and plastic cups. They used a pitcher from home and made their concoction. They also created several signs. Sam and Sally took a folding table from their parents' basement and went down the street to set up in a parking lot, on a corner across from the weekly flea market. They put the signs all around the parking lot, and they were in business.

Unfortunately, they didn't sell many cups right away. Most people got in and out of their cars without giving them much thought. They needed some guerrilla marketing ideas that they could execute cheaply and quickly.

In school, they were studying the U.S. presidents. Sam and Sally quickly drew up a set of trivia questions on small pieces of paper, and put them on the windshield of each car. The drivers were encouraged to go to the lemonade stand to give their answer and get a prize if they won—two cups of lemonade for the price of one. Fortunately for Sally and Sam, most of the adults did not know which number president Millard Fillmore was, but still bought some lemonade.

Sally and Sam learned much about entrepreneurship that day, including management, marketing, sales, operations, and finance. They had to buy the raw materials, find a good location, set a fair price, create signage, market and sell the product, and manage the finances, including profits and losses. The kids also proved to be quite clever at marketing and were able to turn a profit.

I'm sure some of you set up a shop similar to Sally and Sam's in less than one afternoon when you were young. The lemonade stand is a good way to learn a business—for a ten-year-old. But a lemonade stand is not a Cash Machine.

Let's drill down to the reasons for this. First, it's not based on a known skill set. Unless the entrepreneurs had some experience with beverages or retailing, the lemonade stand idea was not based on readily available skills. Second, it wasn't modeled to stand out from the crowd or properly structured to endure. This type of business is not without its competition, nor is it sustainable unless it's legally established and organized. If the lemonade stand is to be a true Cash Machine, the entrepreneurs would need to set up an entity to protect the business. Third, there's no plan, no team, and no acceleration potential. A Cash Machine requires growth in the game plan. This would mean hiring help, changing suppliers to achieve more efficient pricing, borrowing money or getting investors to fuel growth, increasing marketing efforts to include print ads in the newspaper, and eventually franchising the lemonade stand or licensing the name and operating systems to other budding entrepreneurs.

In the ultracompetitive world of beverages, retail, and real estate, this formula for growth seems somewhat unlikely for the little lemonade stand. Unless this type of growth can occur, and more money can be made, the lemonade stand operators will lose interest. Inevitably, the business will take too much time every week as the cost of lemons goes up, but sales don't. Additional problems might occur if a nearby competitor, such as a vendor at the flea market, is pressuring the entrepreneurs with legal action, or if a ruthless competitor has jumped into the fray. Finally, there's no bigger game. It's unlikely that these young entrepreneurs have had time to learn any real business skills in this venture and very likely that the novelty of selling lemonade has worn off. Without business skills firmly in hand, the entrepreneurs cannot move on to the bigger and more interesting game. As a wealth builder, you will always be in pursuit of the better game.

This book delivers a unique and specific methodology for creating a viable, moneymaking enterprise that makes cash fast and leads to financial freedom and wealth. And it all begins with what you already know.

Discover your skills

CHAPTER TWO

Skill Set

Digging into Your Toolbox

Action Plan						
Seven Weeks to Sales						
Week 1	**Week 2**	**Week 3**	**Week 4**	**Week 5**	**Week 6**	**Week 7**
Skills	Idea	Business Model	Revenue Model	Cash Machine Plan	Team	Marketing and Sales

There are two ways to approach entrepreneurship. My technical names for these are the "good way" and the "not good way." Let's start with the latter. The not good way is to start a business in an area that you know nothing about and that requires skills you do not have. The good way is to use the skills you already have to start a business in an area that you know and understand.

Sure, this may seem obvious, but I've seen too many people dive into water that is way over their heads. I ask people all the time what they want to do for a business. Most of the time, the ideas people have for businesses come from their experiences and their dreams of exploiting those experiences, and then doing them better. That's why one of the most common answers to "What type of business do you want to start?" is "I want to start a restaurant." We've all been to restaurants, we all like to eat, and there's something psychologically and culturally rewarding about being the host of an eating establishment, where everyone comes to you, knows your name, and so on. These are similar answers in that vein:

"I want to start a ski shop."

"I can invent a new toy."

"My business will be brownies. I'll have the biggest chain of brownie stores in the world."

Okay. Stop right there. These are not Cash Machines. These are dreams. And while dreams are good, and we'll get to them, they are not your fastest path to cash.

A Cash Machine may or may not be a dream business. Most likely, it is not a cool restaurant or a sports franchise or even a shoe store—unless these businesses take advantage of the skills, experience, and know-how that you already have.

Starting a business is hard enough without handicapping yourself. Most entrepreneurs fail because they choose to pursue entrepreneurship with new skills instead of with known skills. They put their time and energy into an exciting new idea, and rather than learning how to run a business, they end up losing a lot of money, getting exasperated, and giving up. These are not experiences that you want to have. If you can develop business acumen while using skills that you already have, not only will you learn to earn much faster, but you're likely to make money while you're learning. And this is money you can use to launch your dream business later.

Since the first objective of a Cash Machine is to create a business that makes money as soon as possible, right off the bat, there's a chance that the business idea you come up with may not make you giddy with excitement. Take the policeman who wanted to open a sports store. That's a good dream. But his first Cash Machine was a private security business. Or take the techie at a large corporation who had a great idea for a new dog collar. His best chance for building a company that would manufacture and market that dog collar was to first learn to earn by creating a computer consulting business; this was his first Cash Machine. Or take the teacher who really wanted to open a day spa. Her first Cash Machine was a tutoring company. Your moneymaking Cash Machine will lead you successfully and confidently to your dream Cash Machine. Trust the process.

If you already have a business, it's important that you consider whether this endeavor is really working for you as a Cash Machine. Maybe it can create revenue immediately, but the concept just needs tweaking. Or maybe the marketing needs a boost. Perhaps there's a problem with the entity structure. Take a look at your skill set—what you're really good at and what you know—and see if you're putting those tools to their best use. If not, it might be time to create a new Cash Machine. If your current Cash Machine is a dream business, you need to either find a way to make it work as an immediate moneymaker or put it on the shelf until you have fine-tuned your entrepreneurial skills. If it's something in between (you can't give up the business, but it's not making you money), you'll need to get better businesspeople on your team. In Chapter 6, we'll discuss ways for both new and struggling businesses to do this.

Your Current Skill Set

The first step in creating your Cash Machine is just that, creating the Cash Machine. Deciding what your business will be may strike you as somewhat simple, and for many people it is. For many people, however, it's not. In either case, choosing the right business is critical. Of course, you can make a bad choice and begin again, but given that there are so many inherent hurdles to starting a business, it's better to make a good choice from the start. Think of this business decision as you would a potential mate, and hope for a long, healthy, and prosperous commitment to your idea.

There are two notions that can be generated at this juncture. One is the initial Cash Machine, the business that is going to start generating revenue immediately and help you learn to earn. The second is the long-term, entrepreneurial dream.

Amy Arnold was a client we had at one of our Big Tables. The Big Tables consist of groups of 40 to 50 people who spend three weekends with me over the course of a year in order to generate and accelerate their Wealth Cycles. The members of these groups help one another with every aspect of their wealth building, including Cash Machines. Often, there's much brainstorming involved.

Amy was a gym teacher in a private school outside of Atlanta. When she came to the Big Table, we ran through her Gap Analysis. The Gap Analysis includes the Financial Baseline, which is an overview of one's current financial situation, along with the Freedom Day, which states goals and objectives, starting with 120-day objectives and accelerating beyond millionaire status. In this case, Amy's Freedom Day goal was to create a sports foundation that would help teenagers engage in team sports after school.

Amy and her husband, John, owned a house that had appreciated in the past 10 years. They both made a decent living, but each worked long hours, and they had little extra income after taxes. The first step in their Wealth Cycle was the Cash Machine; they needed to make more money and learn to earn. Though Amy's dream of a girls' sports foundation was nice, it wasn't a Cash Machine. The sports foundation would be her second initiative—her long-term entrepreneurial dream. Her Cash Machine would come from the seventh question in the Gap Analysis: "What are the skills you use to make money?"

"I'm a phys ed teacher."

"That's your job," I reminded her. "What are your skills?"

It might not surprise you to learn that a lot of people have trouble understanding what their skill set is. Considering the following scenario might help: *If I picked you up and placed you anywhere in the country, what known skill set could you use to create revenue within a week?*

The answer to that question is your Cash Machine. Whatever the business you come up with, it must generate cash sooner rather than later.

"Well, I manage, and organize, and encourage . . ."

"Good," I said. Amy was on the right path to figuring out her skills.

"I also have to manage the inventory of equipment, oversee ordering and purchases, and my budget for that, and I have to be creative and make up games and drills."

Amy was on a roll; these were the types of skills I was talking about. They would link to management, sales, leadership, organization, marketing, product development, finance, and accounting skills. "And any particular talents?" I asked her.

"I'm a good tennis player," she said. "Tennis is a big sport in our town." Amy lived in a town outside of Atlanta where there were a lot of large, upper-middle-class families. We talked about the number of tennis courts in her town, and how many were privately owned. "Is there any demand for private tennis lessons?"

"Oh, sure," she said. "Parents ask me to refer them to tennis clubs all the time."

"Stop referring them."

"Why?"

"Because you need a Cash Machine, and tennis lessons are going to be your Cash Machine."

"Ha," Amy said. "I don't have time to give tennis lessons."

"You don't have to teach them yourself."

"I don't?"

I shook my head. This is an aspect of Cash Machines that a lot of people don't understand. The point is to create a business that makes money. Hiring other people to do the work can be part of that business. We got Amy on her way to creating a Cash Machine.

Sometimes the correlation between skill set and Cash Machine is obvious. A teacher can create a tutoring business, a Web designer can create a Web design company, and a massage therapist can create a holistic consulting practice. But often the links are less obvious. For example, a mechanic who works at the local gas station might consider an at-home handyman business. Or maybe a high school principal decides to be a life coach. Or a fireman creates safety seminars for families and schools.

Here's a more involved example of creating a Cash Machine.

CASH MACHINE CASE IN POINT

The Music Machine

Jim Stephens, a brand manager for a large consumer products company, and his wife, Dorothy, a music teacher, had a vision to create a music school. For now, this was not their Cash Machine because it could not generate cash immediately or help them learn to earn.

Fortunately, Jim and Dorothy had a lot of skill sets on which to draw. In answer to question 7 of the Gap Analysis, they realized that these skills included marketing, finance, organization, communica-

(continues)

(continued)

tion, and analytics. But additionally, Dorothy had a music skill set, and both Dorothy and Jim had a fondness for helping children.

They decided that their Cash Machine might be voice and piano lessons. They drew up a Revenue Model. In doing this, they decided that they would like to create $5,000 a month in cash flow from the Cash Machine. Since they wanted $5,000 a month, they needed to make $250 a day (20 days in a month, excluding weekends). Then they scouted out other voice and piano teachers in their county and learned that the average price for these lessons was $30 an hour. That meant that they'd need to provide eight or nine hours of instruction a day to hit their gross revenue number. This was too much, given their full-time jobs and the demand that they thought they could generate.

That's when Dorothy's marketing mind kicked in. She'd noticed that there was a trend in the country toward kids starting their own bands. Jim and Dorothy would advertise their idea as an exclusive band-training program. They would have tryouts, place the kids in seven groups of six, and charge each kid that $30 an hour every week. $30 a kid, 4 times a month, times 6 kids per band, times 7 bands, equaled $5,040 a month.

While this met their cash-flow objective, seven hours a week would still take quite a big bite out of their time. That's where Jim's operations skill set came in handy. He decided that they actually needed to be bigger, not smaller. He thought that if they expanded their marketing and the tryouts to the entire county, not just their town, they might easily find more than 42 kids who were interested. If they could increase the number of bands to eight, they'd gross $5,760 a month. They could then use the extra revenue to hire some talented high school kids, at $10 an hour, to run the bands, with Dorothy overseeing the instruction. That $10 per instructor per band would cost $320 a month, allowing Jim and Dorothy to meet their cash flow target without squeezing their time too much.

The start-up cost, in both money and time, would not be insignificant. But once in place, the Cash Machine would

- Feed the Wealth Cycle with cash flow
- Potentially grow and appreciate in value
- Allow Jim and Dorothy to learn to earn
- Provide them with entrepreneurship skills

and, as icing on the cake,

- Move them toward their bigger future vision of a music school

This was a happy day for Jim and Dorothy Stephens.

Finding Your Skill Set

Think about what you do every day at your job. If you already own a business, think about what it is you're doing in the business and whether you are actually capable of doing it. There is a chance that you have a business that does not take advantage of your skills, and that could be one reason you're struggling. Also consider the skills you have outside of your job. We cited the Leonard family in *The Millionaire Maker,* where the father was a mechanic for a heating and air-conditioning company. But during his Gap Analysis, his sons pointed out that he also fixed dune buggies in their garage. This was an important skill set that could not be overlooked and eventually led to the family Cash Machine of making and marketing dune buggies.

If you're not sure about your skills, the following exercise will help you uncover them:

1. List your responsibilities at your job or your company; if you don't have a job, or you have the job of being a full-time parent, list the things you do every day to manage your life.
2. List the specific tasks associated with these responsibilities.
3. List what other tasks you do at your job or to manage your life because either you like to or feel compelled to do them, even though they are not your responsibility.
4. List the industries and markets in which you have experience.
5. List the tasks you do at home.
6. List the activities you find yourself doing in your spare time.
7. List the activities you would choose to do in your spare time.
8. List the tasks that others often ask you to help them with.
9. List the tasks you're good at and might take for granted.

Finding these answers may take some time, but it's worth doing. The success of your Cash Machine depends on a business idea that is in line with your skills. The list might be long or short; it doesn't matter. Sometimes it's almost easier to have fewer skills because it limits your choices. Either way, you will find some skill that can be a Cash Machine. I've never met anyone who can't.

Sometimes the skill set is obvious. Marilyn Stanley found her skill set fit right in her job. She was a graphic designer, and her skill set included graphic design and experience with the Internet; her Cash Machine was going to be a Web site design company. Sometimes it's not so obvious. Al Cypress's skill set was clinical psychology, along with interpersonal skills and an affinity for sports. Through his experience with his business, Al realized that he did not have organization or management in his toolbox. He was on the verge of giving up his business because it was just too much of a hassle. We ran through the assessment with him.

The Skill Set Analyzer	
The Directive	**Al's Answers**
List your responsibilities at your job or your company	"Manage clients, their care and their accounts. Also marketing to get new clients."
List the specific tasks associated with these responsibilities.	"Management, organization, communication."
List the other tasks you do at your job, even though they are not your responsibility, because you like to, or feel compelled to, do them.	"Duties—I have to clean up, because I don't have a janitor. Interests—I like marketing and thinking up new ways to motivate athletes. I like this more than meeting with them."
List the industries and markets in which you have experience.	"Sports, mental health."
List the tasks you do at home.	"Clean the gutters, mow the lawn, fix small things."
List the activities you find yourself doing in your spare time.	"What spare time? Sleeping, watching sports."
List the activities you would choose to do in your spare time.	"Watch more sports, play more sports."
List the tasks others often ask you to help them with.	"Fix things, like hanging curtains, putting up pictures, or small plumbing things. I'm handy with that kind of thing."
List the tasks you're good at and might take for granted.	"Motivating others."

Al's skill set was interesting in that he had narrowed the toolbox he'd learned as a sports psychologist into one skill: one-on-one clinical psychology. Because this skill was volume-sensitive, Al had only so much capacity to generate more revenue. He was dealing with a ceiling on how much business he could do. That is never a good thing for a Cash Machine that needs to accelerate. His answers to the checklist revealed that he might have the potential to create some other products and services that would allow him to increase his revenue without capping out his time. These might include products such as motivational tapes or services such as team therapy or seminars.

Rosa Brackett was also a tough nut to crack as far as her skill set went. A widow who had raised five children, she had never held a job outside of the home. To her surprise, she discovered that her skill set was much wider than she thought. Mothers who stay at home and manage a household tend to have a huge range of skills that they take for granted. These include management, organization, communication, health care, emergency procedures, psychology, creativity—well, you get the picture. I even knew a woman who had no work experience at all who got into one of the top MBA programs in the country by using her stay-at-home-mom skill set as her résumé. Sometimes, it's just perspective. You may know much more than you think you know. Your experience, no matter what it is, is not to be underrated.

You may also want to look at activities and life experiences you had as a child or adolescent in order to uncover your skill set. These may include

- After-school and summer jobs
- Hobbies
- Clubs
- Chores
- Businesses

You might recall that you had quite a productive babysitting business when you were 15, and you might remember that you were very good with children, as well as with managing their parents. Or you may recall the house-painting company you started in college, the summer swimming lessons you gave, or the papers you (legally) helped fellow students to write.

Once you have uncovered the skills that will help you with your Cash Machine, you are well on your way to brainstorming business ideas that use these skills. But first, let's also consider some other skills that you'll want to rely on. In building the Cash Machine, there are three types of skill sets to consider:

- Skills you have
- Skills you are going to need
- Skills you will learn

The Entrepreneurial Skill Set				
Management	Marketing	Sales	Operations	Finance

Characteristics of an Entrepreneur

There's a reason why every single person doesn't go out and start her or his own business, and it's more than the hard work involved. Let's face it, there's something cozy and painless about going to a job every day. Even if you're on the 6 A.M. to 2 P.M. shift at the auto factory, getting dirt under your nails and standing on your feet all day, at least you don't have to think about that work after you walk out the door, and your weekends are yours. There's also the camaraderie of others, the steady paycheck, the benefits, and sometimes there's even a snack room with licorice and good stuff like that.

But let's face the facts. This way of living does have risks. Start with the camaraderie of others. Some of those people might be quite annoying and stifling, and you're stuck with them. As far as the steady paycheck and benefits go, if you've talked to anyone at Delta, General Motors, or Enron lately, you know that stability lives in the 1950s, not now. And I'm sure not every company has licorice, let alone a snack room.

What it takes to break away from the good old W-2 job and start your own venture is a curious mix. Obviously, an entrepreneur needs a different set of skills, including personality and psychological traits, from the W-2 earner. Even your own mental conditioning can hold you back. Once too often you may have heard your mother suggest that you "Get a good government job." Perhaps your father recommended a professional career: "Be a doctor or lawyer, kid; trust me, that'll be good for you."

As different as the skills and personality, psychology, and conditioning of an entrepreneur may seem to be, I firmly believe that anyone who wants to be an entrepreneur can be. If you think certain mental or behavioral aspects of an entrepreneur are beyond you, that's okay. In the Cash Machine, you get to *strengthen your strengths and hire your weaknesses.*

Every single person who starts a Cash Machine, even those who are born to earn, needs a team. I can't say it enough—team, team, team. The best visionaries are also good leaders, and good leaders collect and lead teams. Mavericks who run from the company climate because they want to Lone Ranger their way to glory are rarely successful. As with all wealth-building exercises, you cannot go it alone. Team building is constantly and consistently one of the necessities of being a successful entrepreneur.

Before you get into your Cash Machine, you're going to want to know what is required of you. Let's clarify what skills you need to focus on, perhaps get back into shape, or collect through team members. The most important thing to consider is that when you commit to a Cash Machine, you are making a commitment to shift your thinking and change your mindset. The psychology of a wealth builder who is taking on a Cash Machine cannot be overlooked. Chances are it will take an effort to develop into who you have to be.

To run a Cash Machine, you must *be the business owner.* You have to think like a business owner; you have to act like a business owner; you have to take charge of your life. You need to branch out from any narrow thinking you might have and add some skills to your life. Believe it or not, this is as easily done as said—once you commit to it. You can do this. I've watched hundreds of wealth builders transform before my eyes as they take on a Cash Machine and take charge. It's a fabulous thing to see.

Skills and Personality of an Entrepreneur

No two entrepreneurs are alike. But then again, they're all similar in so many ways. There are certain skill sets and personality traits that you see in every entrepreneur. In listing these attributes, the difference between people with ideas and people who actually can execute their ideas becomes quite clear. An idea person tends to be creative, excited, energetic, hopeful, and constantly stimulated. Yet, while these traits are part of the entrepreneur's repertoire, they are only a small part. Sometimes, it takes only a nice, long walk to come up with a good idea. It always takes hard work and the following skills to make that good idea a good business.

It takes no small amount of *courage* to get up every single morning, day after day, and attack old problems, as well as face new ones. Courage literally means to have heart. There's no better description of what it takes to create something new. A big part of courage is

47

owning one's direction, feeling the pull of where you're going and holding onto that with faith in yourself.

Though you may find yourself doing something new, that doesn't mean it is new to everyone, so be *resourceful.* A smart Cash Machine is built on the brains and sweat of previous research and experience. This comes in handy when we look at modeling the work of others and gathering professionals with experience to uncover the straightest line from where you are to where you want to be.

That straight line requires adopting the proper *perspective:* taking the right steps at the right time. This is *sequencing.* Those who can see what to do when, based on a big-picture view of the entire situation, are the most efficient and effective entrepreneurs. This quality includes using a skill called *future pacing.* Future pacing requires that you see several steps ahead to the goal, then work back to the best steps to take today.

No one but you can make that first phone call to acquire that first team member, find that all-important mentor, or research the market opportunities. It takes *initiative.* Shy is not going to fly in the world of the Cash Machine. Networking, reaching out to others, and jumping in to solve whatever problems need to be solved are obligations. The Cash Machine requires a certain amount of *initiation energy.* This is the amount of focus, drive, and intent that it takes to get the Cash Machine going. And it takes both time and money. If you believe in your idea and are committed to it, you'll be able to devote the necessary amount of initiation energy.

There's only one quality that will ensure that you get what you want, and that's *persistence.* If you have the endurance to persist, the conviction of your vision, and the commitment to your plan, you will eventually reach your goal. This age-old adage, however, has been confused with stubbornness, and that gets a lot of entrepreneurs into trouble. While you have to go at it and be dogged in your persistence, you must also adapt to the world around you. You can have perspective and still be persistent.

This leads to *flexibility.* Staying fluid in your perspective while being persistent enough in your pursuit means that you have to be flexible. This doesn't mean being indecisive or pliable. It means hanging on to your plan, but not getting stuck. Getting stuck stands in the way of getting to your goals. You cannot get stuck. If you hit a snag in the plan, you need to step back from the situation, get a new view, and pivot off in a more productive direction.

Taking *action* cannot be taken for granted. If you spend too much time plowing through research, or analyzing numbers, or having one mentor lunch after another, you'll find yourself doing research, analyzing numbers, or having lunch. The Cash Machine relies on action. If you don't make it your responsibility to actually *do* something, you won't.

Psychology and Conditioning of an Entrepreneur

Entrepreneurs tend to have a certain psychology. It's rare, for instance, that you'll run into a pessimistic entrepreneur. That just wouldn't make sense. There's a faith and belief that is necessary if you are to start your own venture. Of course, if you're reading this book, then you've already placed yourself in this group of the optimistic. You know that there's more for you out there and that with a little direction and a plan, you can get it.

There's a good chance, too, that this psychology comes from one of two places, known as your mother and your father. You can't help it; you are conditioned as a child to think a certain way. Sometimes the traits that parents pass on are perfect for entrepreneurship, and sometimes they are not. Your current conditioning comes either from your childhood or from overcoming that childhood. In pursuing a Cash Machine, you need to adopt the psychology of a successful entrepreneur. If you already have these traits, don't take them for granted. Nurture and build them; you'll need them. If you don't have these traits, find them, either in yourself or in others on your team.

There's no getting around it, you've got to want success if you are to achieve it; you need to have *ambition*. Don't apologize for wanting a bigger, better life. The bigger your life, and the wealthier you are, the more good you can do.

Though ideas may be inspiring, the fact of the matter is that people follow people who are enthusiastic and optimistic. *Enthusiasm* is endearing, and a good leader shares that quality with his or her team. Obviously, this means that you have to experience this enthusiasm at your very core. Somewhere in your genetic makeup—in your core conditioning—you have to have been given a sense of security and love that allows you to believe in yourself and others. Beware, though. At the edge of optimism sits delusion. Grandiose illusions are the empty calories of the entrepreneurial food group. There's a quick rush of excitement, but soon the sugar high wears off and everyone is the worse for wear. *Optimism* that's set in a realistic, believable framework is the most compelling.

When I was seven years old, I was uncomfortable at the kids' table at our Thanksgiving holidays. Encouraged by my Aunt Bev, I just stood up and moved over to the big table, where all the adults were. And I've never left. I've always believed that we all have the right, and even the obligation, to move ourselves to the big table. That's why my workshops are called Big Tables. Too many people spend their lives at the little table, waiting to be served. The Cash Machine prompts you to serve yourself; it develops deservedness, which means that you need to feel that you deserve more.

If you don't believe in yourself, no one else will believe in you; you need *confidence*. Self-doubt keeps too many good people down. While a little doubt is good because it helps you maintain the checks and balances on yourself, too much doubt is like debt in that it can stop you in your tracks. If you don't come by confidence naturally, then you need to get a few cheerleaders on your team. As long as these people are realistic, they can help keep you going when you can't rev yourself up. Many business decisions come down to a gut feeling. It takes confidence to trust your gut. If you don't trust your gut, you're overlooking a valuable asset in your personal arsenal. Believe in yourself and what your stomach tells you. You're here for a reason, and there's no one better than you to make your life better than it is.

The perfectionist is never going to believe that he or she is good enough. Rarely does the perfectionist find satisfaction in any task, even the smallest of steps. This can kill a Cash Machine. If you have confidence, then you can find *satisfaction* in the 80 percent you accomplish without dwelling on that final 20 percent. Getting the task done is more important than getting it done perfectly.

CASH MACHINE CASE IN POINT

The Inconspicuous Skill Set

Amy Arnold, the phys ed teacher who wanted to create a sports foundation, was stalled. Between her work and her family, she didn't have a lot of time. She'd already looked into restructuring some of her lazy assets, specifically some blue-chip stocks, into more aggressive investments. Amy hoped that might be enough to get her Wealth Cycle going. It wasn't. Every Wealth Cycle must have a Cash Machine.

But Amy couldn't quite get it together. As far as her skill set was concerned, she felt pretty good about it. She tended to be resourceful and persistent, and her experience with students had made her flexible. She also was not a perfectionist. In her world, the task just had to get done, and perfect was a distant memory. If asked, she would describe herself as confident, but on the other hand she didn't feel altogether courageous. She knew that she'd have to work on her

(continues)

(continued)

initiative and her perspective, as well as her ability to take action. We talked a bit about her deservedness, and I was sure that this was an ambitious, optimistic, and hopeful person.

Amy's Cash Machine would be private tennis lessons. Aware of her skills and her psychology, Amy knew that she just needed to start learning what she needed to learn. And she'd use her skills to do it:

Courage. Amy was too optimistic and competitive not to go for it. And she believed that she'd succeed.

Resourcefulness. Aware of her time constraints, Amy called a few of her friends and acquaintances with whom she played competitive tennis. She asked them if they'd like to teach. Four of the dozen she called were interested.

Perspective. Amy outlined the plan and saw that she needed coaches, supplies, facilities, and marketing to get students. Spring was three months away, and Amy made a three-month plan to acquire four students for every teacher by the end of April.

Initiative. Amy needed to see how others had done the same thing. She went on the Internet to find private tennis coaches in towns far enough away so as not to be competitive. She talked to several on the phone and signed up for a lesson with two of them. After the lesson, she asked if they'd have coffee, and that's when she conducted an informational interview about their models.

Persistence. Getting the coaches and the mentors and business models happened easily enough, but the students were another matter. Amy expanded her marketing efforts, adding flyers and a Web site to the newspaper ads with which she'd begun her efforts.

Flexibility. After 30 days, Amy still had no clients signed up, and her coaches were getting restless. Many had saved the time on their spring schedules, and they didn't want those days to go to waste. Additionally, the facilities she'd reserved were itching for a down payment. Amy decided to change her strategy. She would provide the lessons on private tennis courts. She found two, one owned by one of her coaches and one owned by a friend. Amy would pay them on a usage basis and stay off the courts when the families wanted them. She also changed her marketing plan. Amy offered a free tennis clinic. She rented an indoor facility, paid her coaches to come, and sent word out through a big display ad in the local newspaper. Dozens of people showed up, and the clinic was a success. Of those attending, several signed up for lessons that spring, and Amy exceeded her client goal.

Amy accomplished all of this by using skills that she already had: resourcefulness, perspective, initiative, persistence, and flexibility. And like the lion in *The Wizard of Oz,* she also discovered one that had been there all along, courage.

The Skills You Learn as You Earn

You need to learn or strengthen the following skills, or *hire* them until you learn to do them. Or, as I have said, strengthen your strengths and hire your weaknesses.

Organization

If you don't have the skill of being organized now, you will get it very quickly as you pursue your Cash Machine. There is just too much to do in a new business venture. Getting it right is tough enough without making mistakes because of clutter and mess. You will learn how to create the proper systems that will help you manage your company. These will include getting all of your personal and company bookkeeping online; delegating small tasks, both personal and professional, to hourly workers; and structuring your entities so that you can forecast your revenues and expenses to the proper companies. It takes this level of organization to maximize your earnings and grow your business. Effective tax strategies, as one example, rely on organization. The IRS doesn't appreciate your best guess at expenses. We will go over all of these systems and structures in the chapter that covers operations.

Energy Management

Most people call this time management, but time is not the real issue. The real issue is how we use our *energy* in that time. If a task is not getting done, you shouldn't do it. You should hire it. Then it will get done. For instance, spending eight hours a month cleaning your home is not the best use of your time, particularly when you can pay someone $10 or $20 an hour to do it.

Also, if you're not managing your energy and efforts properly, chances are you are allowing one activity to bleed into the next. Entrepreneurs tend to have an aptitude for *compartmentalization.* Each meeting has a focus; each activity has an *intent.* Subject matters, whether personal or professional, cannot carry over from one event to another.

Driving the Outcome

In almost every scenario, an agenda is being served. You can feel that this is cynical, or you can be realistic and make the decision to always drive the outcome of every business meeting and conversation. You will have a Cash Machine plan, and you will spend precious time trying to make that plan succeed. Given all the energy and attention that your personal life should consume, it makes no sense to waste time in your business life. If you're going to have a meeting, make that meeting accomplish what you want it to. Drive the outcome.

Quantitative Analysis

Numbers are a part of business, and there is no getting around that. For some people, that's a good thing, because some people find numbers to be a comfort. These people like the fact that numbers are objective and tangible, and that there are formulas through which you can get actual, concrete answers. For others, numbers are a stumbling block. If this is you, you need to get a numbers person on your team. And you also need to get to know numbers. They're not that bad. They're reliable and consistent, and the more time you spend with them, the easier they are to deal with.

Qualitative Analysis

Seeing the subjective factors that surround the objective ones is the skill that makes or breaks a business. Great management, for instance, is essential for a successful business. Yet it takes more than a résumé to know whether a person is right for your business. Trusting your gut is all about the subjective, the qualitative factors that surround the numbers and the facts. If the data resulting from your research and analysis tell you that there's room for another messenger service in town, that's one thing. But if you've asked around enough to know that clients tend to be ultra-loyal to the one messenger service in town, then you might want to be more subjective in your decision and just say no. Knowing when *not* to act is an important action in itself.

Communication

Businesses are built on relationships, and as most of us know, relationships work best when there is clear communication. Relaying the proper specifications to get the job done right, directing vendors and suppliers, clarifying information, sharing the good news, getting ahead of the bad news, enabling employees, engaging partners, marketing, sales, and so on—these are all directly linked to communication. Writing well and speaking well are tools that no entrepreneur can do without, and both can be learned. Modeling others is an efficient way to improve these skills.

Team Building

A Cash Machine is a team machine. Role models are a great way to see how a good team is built. Leaders may be born, but they can also be made. Latching on to good leaders and watching what they do to sell their vision is a great way to learn leadership and team building. Some of these role models might make good mentors and be willing to come aboard your team as consultants or colleagues. You'll also need other colleagues and professionals to assist you with your strengths and fill in for your weaknesses. Support players like administrative assistants and utility players such as a bookkeeper or a graphic designer flesh out the team, as do life support people, such as housekeepers and nannies. Teamwork pervades every inch of the Cash Machine. You need to do a good job of team building to have a working Cash Machine.

Intuition

It might seem funny to view this as a skill, but believe me, reacquiring this innate knack is indeed a skill. Though we are all born with intuition, somehow, along the way, we start to question this gut feeling. I've found that it is this gut feeling, knowing at a cellular level, that can often be my most helpful leadership characteristic. There have been many times when my final decision on a deal came down to trusting my gut, and it has always served me well. Intuition is a form of listening. In fact, intuition is the highest form of listening; it's a general vibe that you can "hear" in almost any situation.

When intuition is working at its best, you can almost anticipate what is going to happen in the room. I've seen many good and effective leaders look at numbers, inspect operations, and then, finally, make the decision with a lot of help from their gut. Experience informs intuition. That's why it is so important to take action and gain experience, so that you can get to a level of listening that makes you a better leader.

Be *on* Your Business, Not *in* Your Business

A good entrepreneur is a leader who has the character and the credibility to create a vision, get others to see that vision, and follow the vision through to realization. In order to do that, you need to be sure that you're *on* your business and not *in* your business.

If you are *on your business,* you are viewing your Cash Machine from above and around. You know where you're going and what it will take to get there from whatever point you're at. You're usually several steps ahead of the current operations and goings-on, and you are aware of who is doing what and when and how their steps fit into the whole.

If you are *in your business,* you are so stuck in the details and day-to-day operations of the venture that you have no idea what the intentions or consequences of your actions are. You can't be both a general and a foot soldier. It just doesn't work. While you need foot soldiers to do the work and advance, you need someone at the map who knows the objective.

Leaders who are on their business tend to future pace. They guide the ultimate direction of the company by viewing its daily operations from where it is supposed to be headed. While you lead your Cash Machine, you should always have a vision of what and where it should be firmly planted in your mind. Then, through reverse technology, you should sequence back from that point in time to create steps to where you are now. In this way, your current actions will pull you toward your goals. This also helps you to stay proactive and not be reactive. Leaders who react to the world around them do not stay leaders for long.

It is your job to anticipate the climate around your Cash Machine and send your company in a direction where it benefits from the movement of the world around you. Reactive leaders are constantly playing catch-up, and there's nothing less productive than that. If you future pace, you should have a good sense of what it will take to steer your Cash Machine in the right direction.

As a leader, you will look down the road for various intervals, from months to years, so that you get a sense of all the signposts. For each date, or marker, you should

- Outline each of your products and/or services.
- Define the market proposition of each of these products and/or services.
- Quantify a target revenue and cash flow for each of these offerings.
- Jot down the strategies and tactics that will support these targets.

This is the final section in the Cash Machine plan because you're going to future pace as soon as you begin thinking of an idea for your Cash Machine. By future pacing early on, you save yourself a lot of time and aggravation. In this day and age, the world moves pretty fast. Though you may have your product or service out of the gate and off and running in 24 hours, you need to continuously anticipate where it's going so that you don't wake up one day and discover that the idea has suddenly become obsolete.

CASH MACHINE CASE IN POINT

The Disappearing Market

Sam Nightingale was a college student who created storage cases for CDs. They were made of a sturdy, natural fabric on which the customers could print with a permanent marker. Most of the material was made from bean bags that the local coffee stores threw out. Sam had the product ready to go a few days after he thought of the idea. He positioned the cases as perfect for music mixes, and soon they were selling like hotcakes in the dorms. Sam sold dozens the first week, and a month later, the number was in the hundreds.

But, a week later, Sam's sales dried up. He'd changed nothing in his product or strategy, and he felt that he'd hardly even tapped the market. Unfortunately, MP3s and iPods were taking over, and no one on campus was making CDs anymore. His product was dependent on the CDs, and with that, his idea became obsolete.

If Sam had looked at the trends and paid attention to the future of the industry, he might have come up with an idea that would have kept him in business.

Future pacing requires sequencing: doing the right thing at the right time. Leaders who can see the right steps are way ahead of the game. This also allows leaders to be efficient and make their highest and best use of time. If you are dredging your way through details or floating around in your dreams, then you're not making your best use of time. Both of these tendencies can be altered by future pacing.

But even the best of leaders can get spun around. That's why it's important to have mentors and coaches who will help you stay on track. Mentors and coaches, by the way, should not just know *how* to do what you're trying to do; they should have actually *done it.* Theory is interesting; experience is helpful. By creating a sequence of doing the right thing at the right time and sharing that sequence with your team, you create an accountability for yourself and your business, as well as a safety net for your decision making. If sequencing is not a skill that you have yet, you need to get someone who has that skill on your team. The best Cash Machine can sink if its leader can't see the next step.

These are just some of the skills you will learn as you pursue your Cash Machine. As you move forward, you are going to get tied up in the business. Step back once in a while; take a moment and reflect on what you are learning Absorbing all of these skills and making them your own is the only way you'll be able to move from your immediate Cash Machine to your ultimate dream Cash Machine.

Once you've listed your skills, it's time to come up with an idea.

Generate a
business idea based
on your skills

CHAPTER THREE

Idea Generation

Brainstorming the Business

Action Plan						
Seven Weeks to Sales						
Week 1	**Week 2**	**Week 3**	**Week 4**	**Week 5**	**Week 6**	**Week 7**
Skills	Idea	Business Model	Revenue Model	Cash Machine Plan	Team	Marketing and Sales

Whether you are building, fixing, or buying a Cash Machine, you need to generate or solidify the idea of the business. This idea will come from your skill set. If you are building a Cash Machine, the business is developed from a set of skills you have. If you already have a business that needs fixing, it probably has a flaw or two that is keeping it from being the optimal Cash Machine. As we've defined a Cash Machine, the business should

- Regularly and consistently generate cash
- Be properly protected and structured
- Utilize an experienced team to reduce risk
- Have growth and acceleration capacity

The important thing is to make sure that your business has sufficient potential. The idea generation stage is a good time to revisit your skill set and ensure that the business you have chosen revolves around your strengths. By getting the business idea in line with what you already know how to do, you'll make more money and have the time and energy to learn how to run the new and improved business properly.

If you are buying a Cash Machine, what you buy should fit in with your skills. Your goal is to get in on an ongoing operation immediately so that you can learn the entrepreneurship skill set more efficiently. In these cases, there is a chance that you don't have any skills that fit in with the ongoing business. For example, you might consider buying a car wash, but you have no skill sets involving cars, heavy machinery, or cleaning. Additionally, you don't bring any of the entrepreneurial skill sets, such as sales, marketing, finance, or operations, to the table. Given that you will be immersed in this operation, you should target a sector or industry that you generally like or are interested in and that might, in some way, fit in with some skills you have. You may know nothing about cars or cleaning machines, but you might be highly organized and excellent with people, so that the systems and customer service aspects of the business have a chance of being supported and improved by what you bring to the table.

This seems like a good place to note that you do not want to build or buy an entrepreneurial venture in the same sector as your investments. If you are heavily invested in real estate, for example, and you are also creating a Cash Machine in real estate, you are putting a lot of your eggs in one industry. The Cash Machine is another opportunity to diversify your asset allocation. If that example hit close to home and you are set on doing your Cash Machine in real estate, consider a 1031 exchange. According to the Internal Revenue Service Code Section 1031, if you exchange business or investment property solely for business or investment property of a like kind, no gain or loss is recognized. And so you might want to consider a 1031 exchange of some of your real estate investments into other like-asset classes, such as oil and gas or an equity venture that has property attached to it.

Hitting on an idea may or may not seem that difficult to you. As I've said, though, the goal is not to come up with just any idea; it's to arrive at a *good* idea. In order to find the right venture—one that's not only interesting, but real—you may need a little help in the thinking department. Idea generation is a good time to start casting around for team members. Once you've discovered your skills, find a mentor and ask for business ideas. Everyone likes to give advice, and reaching out to a mentor for ideas is a good step toward getting that mentor on your team.

Just as two heads are better than one, several ideas help spur the best of ideas. That's why brainstorming is a great idea-generating tool. The way to keep the ideas pouring out is by not filtering them. Let all the ideas flow, even the absurd ones. You never know. If someone throws into the air the idea that because you're good with animals, you should breed and sell some new weird pedigree, that might spark the idea in someone else's head to start a special kennel and dog-walking service for Labradoodles.

Heading the Right Way

Once you are committed to action, things move pretty quickly in the sequence of steps to start up the Cash Machine. It's important, then, to first make sure that your idea gets you going in the right direction. To understand that direction, you should ask yourself three questions:

1. What do you want?
2. What are you committed to?
3. What is possible?

Knowing what you want will keep you on track and help to focus your mind on creation. Making a commitment will give you clarity, because it is this *commitment* that helps you access the know-how that will go toward fulfilling your goals. Commitment helps you put together the team you want, and this team will help you work through the tough stuff and create accountability for action.

The 120-Day Plan

The process of getting to the right idea should not cause analysis paralysis. The goal is to embark on immediate action so that you can start gaining experience that will deliver the evidence you need to build the confidence that will get results.

Action ➠ Experience ➠ Evidence ➠ Confidence ➠ Results

After you brainstorm, you need to get moving. The 120-Day Plan gets you out of analysis and into action. The moment you put something into a schedule, you've created the time for it. Schedules create accountability and responsibility. These schedules are for the entire Wealth Cycle and cover asset allocation and investing, as well as the Cash Machine. The part that is pertinent for the Cash Machine looks like this:

Loral's 120-Day Wealth Cycle Plan				
From:		**To:**		
Goals:				
1.				
2.				
3.				
4.				
Month #1				
Tasks for Goal #:	Week #1	Week #2	Week #3	Week #4
1.				
2.				
3.				
4.				
Month #2				
Tasks for Goal #:	Week #1	Week #2	Week #3	Week #4
1.				
2.				
3.				
4.				
Month #3				
Tasks for Goal #:	Week #1	Week #2	Week #3	Week #4
1.				
2.				
3.				
4.				
Month #4				
Tasks for Goal #:	Week #1	Week #2	Week #3	Week #4
1.				
2.				
3.				
4.				

Follow the seven weeks to sales schedule. Choose a specific date, before or at seven weeks from day 1 and idea generation, to begin the business. Mark it on your 120-day calendar: "Revenue into Cash Machine Begins." This will be the day that you get your first client or customer through marketing. You are going to work backward from this date. With that objective on the very near horizon, you will be motivated to get going. You also want to set up objectives for the entire four-month period. Tasks to accomplish in this time period include

- Idea generation
- Calling mentors
- Modeling businesses
- Preparing revenue models
- Team building
- Contracts for the team
- Entity structuring
- Marketing and sales activities
- Generating sales leads and cultivating prospective clients
- Setting revenue targets

We've also created a 120-day table on which you can list the specific tasks you need to perform to get to each of these goals.

Loral's 120-Day Plan				
From:		**To:**		
Goals:				
1.				
2.				
3.				
4.				
Goal #	**Tasks**	**Start Date**	**End Date**	**Comments/ Resources**

As you can see, the table begins with a list of specific goals for that four-month period. It then lists each and every task that needs to be done. Though this can seem a bit detailed, it's important to write down exactly what needs to happen. This will help you outline all the steps in the sequence and accomplish each one. There are also columns for start date and end date; this creates accountability. The dates on the tasks list should match those on the calendar.

Obviously, the Cash Machine requires that you track your numbers, dates, and tasks meticulously. This keeping track helps you to keep control of what you are doing and when it will happen. Once you commit to each task, write down how many times a week you are going to perform that task. Write these plans in ink, make the commitment, and be accountable. I can't overstate how helpful writing down action items is for accomplishing tasks and eventually reaching your goals.

This type of planning supports the *action* requirement of a Cash Machine. The objective is to make a plan and commit to that plan. Though it may seem tedious, it's an important part of the process. By putting it in writing, you are taking the first action step.

Of course, the idea must come first.

The Current Climate

There are several factors that you might want to consider while thinking of your business. These factors will help you both trigger ideas and see if they are viable.

The Market Opportunity

Consider what's missing in your town or community. Most likely, this will be something that's been on your radar for a while. While there may be several holes in your local market, these opportunities are good business ideas only if they fit into your skill set. If your area lacks day care and you have a lot of experience with children, as well as creativity, organization, time management, and patience, this is a good Cash Machine for you. Likewise, your area may have a pizza place that's less than desirable, yet everyone eats there anyway and just complains about it. That's a business that's ripe for being bought. However, you don't have any skills involving food, or entertainment, or service, or organization, and what's worse, you're allergic to cheese. Furthermore, you've no access to any team that can cover for you with these skills. This is a Cash Machine opportunity, but not for you.

Trends

Everywhere you look, you see . . . what? Maybe it's a need for Web sites, or moving companies, or interior design, or landscaping. As demand grows, supply sometimes can't keep up. You might be able to build, fix, or buy a Cash Machine that grabs on to the coattails of an already established, very good idea. Let's say you own a beauty salon that's fighting to find customers every week. You overhear your clients complaining that they can never get an appointment at the laser hair removal place. Adding this service to your product line might be a good business idea that will upgrade your business and transform it into a Cash Machine. It's no accident that where there's a McDonald's, there's a Burger King. The entrepreneurs of Burger King realized that there was enough demand to go around, and since the McDonald's folks had already done the legwork to find the best high-traffic locations, putting a restaurant across the street saved a lot of time on wheel reinvention.

Whispers

Sometimes, you might find yourself ahead of the market opportunity and the emerging trends. These are special opportunities that are not to be taken for granted. If you work at the Chamber of Commerce and you hear rumblings about a new mall that's going up, and if you happen to have a skill set that revolves around driving and relationships with senior citizens, then the idea of starting a mall limo service from the senior center might be a good Cash Machine.

Parallel Worlds

Many times, things are happening "there" that aren't yet happening "here." Your friend in another town might tell you how she used a local service to hire a high school student to come to her home and install her computer. If your skill set is organization and management and your son's high school friends are spending too many afternoons on your couch in front of the TV, you might be primed for such a Cash Machine. Similarly, you might travel frequently and have noticed a certain demand in Denmark for products and services that aren't offered here, but should be.

Sources for Ideas

There are many resources for digging into the current climate. These include the following:

- *Traditional and new media.* Newspapers, magazines, television, the Internet, cell phones, and other portable devices are obvious sources for learning what's going on. It is important that you keep up with the news and events of the day, if only to know what everyone else is thinking and doing. Obviously the goings-on delivered through the media can be either major or minor. Big or small, you obviously want to latch onto the upswing of a trend. You want to be the person who thinks to sell life rafts in areas that are susceptible to flooding. You don't want to be the one who comes up with selling rug cleaners when the hottest do-it-yourself show is hyping hardwood floors.

- *Pop culture.* As much as it might pain you to pay attention to the latest media offering or store opening or clothing style, these things can help you understand the market and what's being desired, or aspired to, by the masses. Understanding aspiration is no small thing. Martha Stewart built an empire on the desire to establish the perfect household, Phil Knight made millions from athletic ambitions, and Jenny Craig exploited body image perfection when she created her weight loss centers.

- *Trade and research reports.* Industry- and business-specific newspapers, magazines, newsletters, and Web sites are terrific and underutilized sources of information. There is no better place to learn the language and meet the players in certain sectors. Even though most Cash Machines begin as small operations within a big industry, it is helpful to understand the industry you're in. If you're starting a handyman business, but you haven't read any of the home improvement trade magazines, you might not realize that customers tend to get a handyman through word of mouth and won't respond to traditional advertising. Or perhaps you want to create an equipment leasing business. It will help to read brokerage firm research reports and learn that they emphasize cash flow over income in that sector. You'll save time by knowing which numbers you need to focus on in your own business. Trade media are like an invitation to a behind-the-scenes club. These resources help you start talking the talk and walking the walk of any given business. They don't call them trade secrets for nothing.

- *Business broker listings and papers.* If you know you're going to buy your Cash Machine rather than create it, scour the business-for-sale classifieds in general newspapers and in the business broker listings. While there are professionals who are literally business brokers, there are also Web sites and papers called business brokers that are just channels for buying and selling businesses. One click in your search engine and you'll see an abundance of opportunities. Too many. Buying a business is very much like investing in any other asset; it requires the proper due diligence. Though we will look at how to approach these acquisitions, I also suggest referring to *The Millionaire Maker's Guide to Wealth Cycle Investing,* where we dig into due diligence and valuation when acquiring a company.

- *Display ads, commercials, and even the Yellow Pages.* Advertising has always been a great sign of its times. It is also a good source of ideas. Companies don't advertise on a whim. It's an expensive proposition, and they've done their homework before they spend their ad dollars. You can take advantage of all their work. Look at the way they position their product. Notice what audience they seem to be targeting. Try to deduce the demand-supply equation that the company is tapping into. There's a chance that you can tap into a similar demand-supply equation. Skim through magazines, and check out billboards as you drive past. This will get your mind going on what's desirable and who's desiring it. A simple ad on the radio might give you a great idea. The Yellow Pages are another source. If nothing else, because of the alphabetical listing of industries and products that they provide, the Yellow Pages can steer you to an idea within a certain skill set that you might have overlooked. Let's say you know you want to provide some form of bookkeeping. The exact form may come to mind when you scan the various businesses in the bookkeeping section of the Yellow Pages.

- *Field trips.* This is one of my favorite ways to generate ideas. It might be a simple trip across town to see a new Laundromat where business is booming because the owner put in a coffee bar and a pool table. It could be more involved, like a jaunt to another town, state, or even country that may stimulate an idea. It could be a small idea with small potential that's just perfect for that starter start-up. On a visit to Texas, you might have seen your friend go to a local, ad-supported Web site where parents shared comments on children's museums, parks, theater, and activities in Dallas. Realizing that your town has nothing like this, you could export the model for your city or state. It may be a trip abroad that stimulates the idea. In 1979 a businessman named Paul Fireman, who already had experience in outdoor sporting goods, spotted some interesting English running shoes at a trade show. He got the license and later that year introduced the sneakers into the United States under the brand Reebok. That turned out to be a pretty nice Cash Machine.

Spend time scouring as many sources as you can. You never know.

Rules of Idea Engagement

I have three rules for reaching a decision on what form your Cash Machine should take.

1. *Keep it simple.* A Cash Machine is not the same as a traditional entrepreneurial venture in that you must be up and running in seven weeks—at most. This gives you little room to be too clever or to create an idea that is too complicated.

While your eventual Cash Machine may be complex, your immediate Cash Machine should be simple, with a clear and obvious sequence to revenue generation.

2. *The obstacle of original.* There is rarely such a thing as an original idea, and if an idea is *too* original, its chances of acceptance are low. For the most part, we are all exposed to the same stimuli. We can't help it. We live in a world where the media have the ability to inspect and invade almost anything that is going on in this world. Few places or people are out of reach. And most of us who are watching news shows, reading newspapers, or surfing the Internet are viewing and absorbing the same things. That's why you often see similar products lining the shelves, or three movies with the same idea in the theaters at once. It's almost impossible to come up with an original idea. Whatever stimulated you and your thought process probably stimulated six other people at the same time. Trying to be too original will strain your brain and waste your time. Derivative ideas often work best for a profitable initial Cash Machine. Take advantage of what's already been done. You can still strive for originality in certain aspects of your business. That adds flavor, and flavor is fun, but do not spend too much time pursuing originality at the idea stage of your first Cash Machine.

3. *The supply and demand disconnect.* If you can see a big gap between what's available and what's in demand, then you are well on your way to creating a viable Cash Machine. Unfortunately, the opportunity is rarely as obvious as a big gap. Most often it's just a little fissure. But if you can see it, there is probably enough room in which to start a Cash Machine.

I noticed just such a fissure when I started my wealth coaching company, Live Out Loud. Attending seminars for wealth building speakers in order to learn a bit about the field, I became aware of the disconnect between what to do and how to do it. The speakers got the audiences excited about building wealth but left the stage without offering them their support. I also noticed that what little coaching was available came from scripted coaches who offered general, not specific, advice. There was nothing tailored to individual needs, and worse, the advice was theoretical, not practical. I saw the demand for one-on-one personal, tactical, results-oriented wealth coaching. I put my team together, defined the product and service, and in days was generating revenue. My Cash Machine took off all because of a slight, but as yet undiscovered, opening in the marketplace.

Some Ideas to Get You Going

Your team will probably be the best source of ideas and the best walls off of which to bounce your own ideas. I've listed several Cash Machine ideas on www.liveoutloud.com/cmideas, and here are just a few that might help you think of a good business for yourself:

- Handyman-and-mechanical at-home services
- Transportation, moving, and hauling services
- Clutter control and organization for homes and offices
- House design, decorating, or cleaning
- Car care, detailing, and washing
- Tax preparation and returns
- Grant writing
- Event planning
- Exercise and physical instruction
- Silk screening and personalized products
- Recording and video services
- Nutritional products and programs
- Home-cooked meals delivered to the elderly

- Consulting: marketing, finance, operations, retail
- Coaching: sports, music, dance, theater, performance, speech, art
- Tutoring: math, English, science, languages
- Outsourcing: writing, graphic design, bookkeeping
- Specialized crafts: clothes, jewelry, metalwork, woodwork, scrapbooks
- Caretaking: children, pets, seniors, disabled

CASH MACHINE CASE IN POINT

Multiply Ideas and Sales

After Al Cypress thought about his skill set, his view of his own Cash Machine began to change. Though sports psychology was what he knew, the way he was offering it was not the best and highest use of his time. More and more, Al was making special audio files for his clients to use during their workouts. Though each was tailored to an individual client, Al realized that there were similar themes, and he found himself repeating certain insights. He also found that the same themes sometimes worked for different athletes and different sports.

Al created a Web site where he could store the files and to which he could refer his clients. Soon, his clients asked if they could share these files with others. Al then found that the files were becoming popular podcasts.

That's when he decided to change the business model of his Cash Machine. Al hired another psychologist to take over the one-on-one clinical practice. Then he focused on the podcast audio files. He also created videos and other products, such as inspirational training calendars. Al was on his way to working less, marketing more, and creating multiple streams of revenue for his new and improved Cash Machine.

Buying a Business

If you've decided to buy a business, it has to be a Cash Machine. The bowling alley down the street that's been run down for years may be for sale, and it may even be cheap, but if it needs a lot of physical work, the equipment needs to be replaced, and no one in town bowls anymore, then you shouldn't buy it. It's not a Cash Machine. You also don't want to infuse cash into a friend's struggling company, even if it's one that has a great new product idea, but no sales, no customers, and no operations. That would be like creating a whole new company, and not a Cash Machine. The company you buy can't be the remnants of someone else's dream business with no cash-flow prospects.

In buying a business, you are looking for an ongoing business venture that is already making money or is, at the very least, breaking even. If there are clear and obvious opportunities for operating efficiencies, where a few fixes will quickly pump up the revenue and the margins, then that's all the better. Sometimes these operating efficiencies can even reduce your acquisition costs if they are initiated quickly enough.

When you look at potential companies to buy, you don't want to buy a great business with little room for improvement, and you don't want to buy a terrible business with too much room for improvement. You want a good, solid business that is doing fine. The point of buying a Cash Machine instead of creating one is to leapfrog that troublesome struggle-to-get-on-your-feet stage. Buying a Cash Machine should allow you to learn the entrepreneurial skill set a bit faster, without putting you in over your head. Businesses that might be both interesting and helpful as a Cash Machine include the following:

- Car washes
- Coin-operated game arcades
- Convenience stores

- Gas stations
- Hardware and supplies
- Laundromats
- Machinery shops
- Manufacturing operations
- Marinas and RV parks
- Storage

These businesses may or may not seem exciting, but if they have a reliable customer base and a steady stream of revenues, that money in your pocket gets very exciting very quickly. Industries that tend to be a bit more challenging include

- Entertainment
- Fashion
- Food service
- Health and beauty
- Leisure and lodging
- Media
- Recreation
- Retail
- Travel

Some people refer to these as the glamour industries. They are more difficult Cash Machines because they are strongly trend-dependent, customer service–oriented, and time-intensive. You may be running a good operation, but your customers can just dry up for no reason other than that they've fallen in love with another option. Such consumer fickleness happens too often in these areas, and then you're fighting for market share with heavy-duty marketing. Though you may discover a viable Cash Machine opportunity in one of these sectors, and I have, I don't recommend looking here first.

In looking at a business, as with any investment, you have to consider the perspective of the seller. If a plumbing manufacturer has strong sales, has a good customer base, and doesn't need to advertise, you have to wonder why the owner would sell. If you discover that it's because the owner is older and wants to move to a warmer climate, that could be a good reason. If you discover that the owner is just tired of it after two years, there might be some problems with time intensity that you should look into. I have found that too many people tire of owning businesses because they have no concept of maintaining a team. The Lone Rangers get burnt out quickly, and that's a chance for you and your team to drop in and improve the business.

Values

There's no use becoming a millionaire if you have to become someone else to get there. As you brainstorm ideas for your Cash Machine, you want to make sure that what you do is in line with both your values and your vision. Your immediate Cash Machine does not need to work with your ultimate vision, and in most cases it will not. But as with everything you do in generating wealth, your Cash Machines, both the immediate and the ultimate, must fit with your values.

Understanding what these values are is important and is worth a moment of your time. If the environment is high on your list of what's important to you, that will guide your options. Let's say your experience is in food and your skill set includes time management and coordinating operations; a Cash Machine that delivers lunches in Styrofoam containers is not going to work for you. To get you thinking about your own value system, here are examples of values: accomplishment, achievement, advancement, affection, availability, community, cooperation, creativity, education, family, freedom, friendliness, health, honesty, individuality, innovation, integrity, intelligence, justice, kindness, liberty, loyalty, order, originality, peace, power, pride, recognition, spontaneity, self-respect, spirituality, vitality.

Values are peculiar to each person. Community might be very high on your list and individuality somewhat low, whereas another person could have individuality as the number one value and community not even on the radar. You should make a list of your own values and see what's nonnegotiable for you. It may surprise you to discover that you need order and predictability in your life. This will help you weed out any Cash Machine that relies on spontaneity.

Vision

It's important to stay motivated while you build your Wealth Cycle. Some wealth builders find it difficult at the beginning—and for good reason. There's a lot of tedium involved in establishing your Financial Baseline, restructuring assets, gathering a team, establishing entities, and building a Cash Machine—especially if you do not like the options for businesses that your skill set allows. I've heard many teachers tell me that they don't want to start a tutoring business, they'd rather run a resort. My response is to tell them that they will get to do that later, but for now they have to learn to earn and make money with the skills and experience they already have. While that makes sense, sometimes the day-to-day operations can be a bit tiresome.

That is why you need to have a vision of your future, the ultimate Cash Machine toward which you're working. It might be a massive real estate investment company. Maybe it's a nonprofit organization that helps others. It could be a dream you had when you were a kid—an old-fashioned ice cream parlor, a surf shop, a movie production company. Brainstorm ideas for your immediate Cash Machine, and also consider what your eventual Cash Machine will be. This business will be part of your ultimate vision.

No-limit thinking allows for the best of inventions and ideas. In this type of thinking, you conceptualize your ultimate Cash Machine by dreaming big and pushing your wish list. The vision is formed as if there's no chance for failure, allowing you to stretch your ideas so that you stretch your life. Like your Cash Machine, your vision should fit in with your values. Most likely, your vision will change over time. Set it down while you establish your first Cash Machine, and then continuously nurture it in your mind. It's the carrot. This vision should motivate you to learn to earn so that you can eventually live in the world you want.

Model the idea

CHAPTER FOUR

Modeling

Finding a Form to Follow

Action Plan						
Seven Weeks to Sales						
Week 1	Week 2	Week 3	Week 4	Week 5	Week 6	Week 7
Skills	Idea	Business Model	Revenue Model	Cash Machine Plan	Team	Marketing and Sales

To go where no human has gone before was a good mission for *Star Trek,* but it's not so good for the creator of a Cash Machine. Novice entrepreneurs cannot afford to get lost in the months of research and development that creation takes. In the seven weeks you have to get your Cash Machine up and running, the last thing you want to do is reinvent the wheel. Modeling your Cash Machine after a business that already exists is a smart way to hit the ground running.

Getting the Inside Track

Once you have your business idea, you should model a similar business. A look around your area, on the Internet, or in business listings should help you find a venture that's based on an idea like yours. It is best if you can meet the business owners in person, see their operations, or ideally even shadow them for a day. Following entrepreneurs around their operations is a good way to really see what's going on. If you can't get a meeting, a phone call works too, although this should be preceded by your own personal inspection of the product or service.

The level of challenge in finding a business similar to yours depends on the nature of your idea. If you are choosing a service based on a model you saw while you were on vacation, then it's simple: you have your model, and you can make the call. If your product is similar to others that exist, but you have no proximity or access to those businesses, then finding a model will be a little more challenging. Spreading the word about your intentions is one way to find your way to these models.

Once you come up with your idea, I strongly suggest that you share your vision and your thoughts with others. Let's say you want to start a housecleaning venture. You mention this at a party, and a friend of a friend knows the person who started the Easy Maids service three towns over and is willing to connect you. This happens all the time. Speak up about what you're doing. You never know what connections or opportunities may come from a few offhand remarks.

Your contact person within the business does not have to be the owner of the business; any number of people within a company are possible resources. Sometimes the best source of information isn't even in the company at all. Often a strategic partner or retail customer can have a lot of insight into how a particular business works. The important thing is to find the right person, or people, based on a recommendation by someone whose judgment you trust.

Marilyn Stanley knew that many others had gone before her in creating Web site design companies, and she wasn't out to reinvent the wheel. She only wanted to make more money and to learn to earn. She shared her idea for a Web site design company with several people. Eventually, a friend had a friend who would, indeed, be of great help to Marilyn; his name was Adam Allison. Adam had a successful Web firm in Reno, Nevada. He focused on individuals and small businesses. The friend suggested that Marilyn check out Adam's Web site and then make the call.

Marilyn looked at Adam's Web site, and also those of his clients. This gave her a fairly good idea of his business. She then called Adam and asked if he'd mind speaking to her about setting up a business. In the initial communications with companies you hope to model, you should keep the following in mind:

1. Establish the link immediately, so that the individuals know who referred you.
2. Ask if this is a good time to talk.
3. Explain why you are calling: that you are looking to connect with them based on the success of their businesses and your desire to model your own business after theirs.

4. Clarify your intention so that they don't feel threatened by your venture; underscore the fact that you will not be in their market or poach their customers.
5. Keep these first contacts brief.
6. Use the initial call to set up a time to meet or to talk again.

During the next communication, you'll want to perform your due diligence and learn as much as you can about the model business. The 21 questions below will help get you started.

INFORMATIONAL INTERVIEW WITH A MODEL CASH MACHINE

1. What is the product or service that you are selling?
2. To whom are you selling it?
3. What was the opportunity when you created or acquired your business?
4. Was there an opening that you took advantage of?
5. Who were the other players in the market at the time?
6. What were the industry trends then?
7. What are some of the current industry trends?
8. What was (and what is now) distinct or unique about your product or service?
9. How did you (and how do you currently) position your offering differently from those of your competitors?
10. Are there any current gaps between supply and demand of which you are aware?
11. How did you initially market your product or service?
12. How do you currently market it?
13. What were some of the specific challenges that you faced immediately? That you faced eventually? That you face now?

14. Who is indispensable on your team?
15. Do you tend to hire people or offer them equity?
16. What can I expect to charge for services similar to yours?
17. What items represent some of your biggest expenses?
18. Are there any unseen costs that I shouldn't be surprised by?
19. What is your strategy going forward?
20. Do you plan to exit the business at any time? What is your exit strategy?
21. Are there any other successful companies that you would suggest I look at?

Most likely, business owners will not have the time or the desire to answer all of these questions. It's best to do as much research as possible before you meet with business owners. You don't want to waste their time asking about details you could get off the Internet. Additionally, if you know that they are going to allot you only 15 minutes, pick questions that only they can answer. Then ask if they can recommend others in the business who can answer the other questions.

Adam Allison's answers to Marilyn's questions were crucial in forming the plan for her Cash Machine. In fact, some of his comments redirected her initial thoughts. For example, she had been going to target everyone, from individual customers to large corporations. However, when she heard Adam's thoughts on the industry, she realized that small companies were the best target audience. She also learned some of the big land mines for the entrepreneur. One of the biggest, according to Adam, was collecting payment from his clients. This area of finances, accounts receivable, can be a huge issue for a small company and is not to be underestimated. In fact, I've seen companies go under because they couldn't collect from their clients. This drove Marilyn to work with a bookkeeper to create a specific e-mail invoice to help collect payments.

Marilyn was fortunate that Adam not only was generous with his time, but actually understood and could explain his business. This is not to be taken for granted. It might shock you to discover how many people don't really understand their own business. Or if they do, they can't explain it clearly. You will probably find this as you try to model your Cash Machine. There's no need to lose heart; just find several business owners of whom you can ask these questions. The combination of all their answers will help you get yours. If a source of this information is someone you find you admire and like, arrange a person-to-person meeting with that individual and consider bringing that person onto your team as a mentor or consultant.

Close, but No Cigar

There's a chance that you won't be able to find a good model for your idea. You might, however, be able to find a model that's similar enough. In this case, you have to take a different approach to modeling the business.

Consider Al Cypress's idea of fixing his business by focusing on downloadable audio files offering motivational advice to athletes during their workouts. In revamping his Cash Machine Plan, Al had a hard time finding anyone who was doing anything close to what he had in mind. He found several sports psychologists, but they didn't offer alternative products on a Web site. The podcasting sites had a few products that focused on self-help, but not in the scalable, goal-directed way he was doing it. Basically, there was no perfect fit.

This is not unusual. It's quite common to be in the "almost-but-not-quite" category of business ideas. However, Al may have had a horse of a different color, but he still had a horse. He wasn't creating something strange or unfamiliar. Though he couldn't find a direct model, there was no reason that he couldn't find something *similar but different* after which to model his business.

One way to do this is to divide your business idea into different segments and model each of those segments after an easier-to-find business. For the audio files, Al looked at Web sites that offered audio files for sports, psychology, and/or self-help. He then looked at psychologists who had both a clinical practice and a self-help product line, such as books. Al also looked for the exact operational model he was proposing, but in another industry. He was targeting an in-person practice that offered products online. Al found a health and wellness spa that had one-on-one consultations supplemented by product sales. He also looked at a few musicians' Web sites that showed live concert dates and allowed music to be downloaded.

When the businesses out there are not exactly like the idea you have, it takes an ounce more energy and flexible thinking to find a good model. But for most ideas, there is a useful model to imitate.

Outside Looking In

Sometimes there is an obvious parallel business out there, but it is completely inaccessible and you have no hope of talking to anyone associated with it. If the business is based on a very simple idea (and many times the best ones are) and there are obvious models all around you, then you can learn about the business without knowing someone on the inside. If the business is the type you can inspect on your own, get in there and take a look. Not only will you have a chance to see how the operations are set up, but there might be an opportunity to talk to customers, employees, suppliers, and distributors.

Let's say you want to buy a Laundromat, but you can't find a Laundromat owner who is willing to talk to you. You can go to a Laundromat that you consider successful and observe its operations. In your investigation, you can

- Count the machines.
- Check out the pricing.
- Calculate the traffic flow of customers.
- Absorb the patterns of customer usage.
- Absorb the other products and services available.
- Stake out the available parking.

The extent of your investigation can go as far as you want. This research can range from working in the model for a short period, engaging with the model as a customer, or, as in the case of the Laundromat, finding the name of the service provider stuck to the back of the machines and calling to find out about service and maintenance. Take the time to learn as much as possible up front. This is always worth the effort.

Perhaps you are creating a business that fills a need in the market. You've talked to people at similar businesses in faraway towns, but now you want to gather information from potential strategic partners in your area. When I started my personal coaching business, it was important for me to talk to those offering seminars so that I could zero in on what my business would look like and also suggest the idea of joint venturing (a concept we'll discuss in the marketing chapter) my coaching with their seminars. Eventually, I did seminars too, but coaching was a good first step for me, and I learned a lot from the models of those who had gone before me.

Let's say your skill set is gardening and customer relations, and you want to create home delivery of garden products from wholesale distributors and some retailers. A trip to one of the nearby garden centers can be very fruitful. You can get an idea of the type and range of products offered to the same demographic you'd be serving, and you can also attempt to speak to some of the customers and get a sense of the opportunities to be filled in the market.

The garden center's products, services, display, pricing, and promotions are all good indications of how you can model your offering. Once you've done your walk-around and seen how things work, try to get a conversation going with the owner. It's always best to be straightforward about your intentions. Approach the owner with the view that your vision is an opportunity for him. In this case, since he doesn't provide delivery and that's what you want to offer, there's an opportunity for collaboration between the two of you. He could use your service for his customers, and you could recommend his store to some of your clients. Your marketing and sales skills should get a little workout right at the modeling stage as you try to enroll these potential strategic partners.

Revenue Modeling

Of all the businesses you can consider, the best model is a bigger, better version of your concept. Marilyn Stanley decided that Adam Allison's company was what she wanted hers to be. Through her conversations with him, she uncovered his concept, market, and strategies. She also came to understand the structure of his financials. Adam's pricing and volume strategies for making money were necessary components of *revenue modeling,* the calculation that Marilyn needed to do in order to determine whether she had a viable business.

Businesses run on the numbers. If you don't make money, there's no reason to run the business. You have to forecast the numbers to see if your Cash Machine is even doable. The Revenue Model is an analysis that projects how much money you will make in a certain period. This number becomes a commitment, and all of the strategies for the business revolve around this target. Whether you are building, fixing, or buying a business, the Revenue Model is a tool for setting goals and establishing the viability of a business concept.

This commitment to a number is the key to the Revenue Model. It's not a projection of what you *can* make; it's a projection of what you *will* make. Consider how much money you have committed to make, and then determine what it will take to hit that target. This drives you to understand exactly what you need to do to make those numbers, and as a result the business, work. Getting the business up and running and making a profit is no big deal; that's just a lemonade stand. Getting to target numbers and making more and more money as you grow—that's a Cash Machine.

CASH MACHINE CASE IN POINT

Revenue Modeling

Bob, an administrative assistant, wanted to create a Cash Machine. His skill set was organization and communication, and he decided that his business concept was to provide a "personal assistant service to organize and maintain finances, filing, databases, and scheduling." Bob wanted his Cash Machine to generate an extra $1,200 a month, just to get started. His goal to get there, then, was to charge $25 an hour and get three people who needed four hours a week each. When he got those clients, he was taking in $300 a week and $1,200 a month.

Goal	Rate	Hours	Clients
1,200/month	$25/hour	12 hours/week	3/week × 4 hours each

Bill, an accountant at a large firm, called a few independent accountants to find out what services they provided and how much they charged. He discovered that he could charge about $500 for preparing and executing personal tax returns, mostly during the months of January, February, March, and April. Bill started a Revenue Model. First, he decided that he'd like an additional $10,000 a year, to get started. This meant that he needed to do at least 20 personal tax returns. This seemed doable to him.

Goal	Rate	Projects	Clients
10,000/year	$500 per project	20	5/month × 4 months

Betty, a jewelry designer, had Wish Now gem bracelets that she wanted to sell at her local outdoor market. She shared a table with a friend every Saturday and paid the friend a fee from her sales. Betty wanted to make an extra $2,000 a month in revenue (before the fee to her friend). She would do this by making $500 every Saturday. She priced the bracelets at $50 each and made a goal to sell 10 at each market.

Goal	Price	Products
$2,000/month	$50 per product	10/week

In these examples, we gave you three different ways of performing revenue modeling. None are that difficult. Simple and practical are the themes of the Cash Machine. Running a business is enough work; doing the analysis and research beforehand shouldn't be overwhelming.

Hitting $100,000

The target revenue number I always use in my Big Table seminars is $100,000 a year. Now remember, your eventual goal for a Cash Machine is not $100,000 a year. That's not enough. It's just not worth putting all of the time and energy into creating a new business to get $100,000. You might as well work yourself to the bone in a corporation for that salary. And anyone who says, "Yeah, but isn't it great to be working for yourself" has never run his own business. Just because you work for yourself doesn't mean you work for yourself. When you have your own company, you are working for investors, the bank, your employees, your partners, and every single customer who calls to complain about this or that. Believe me, it's not worth it for $100,000 a year.

I chose $100,000 as the target revenue example because when you begin your Cash Machine, you will still have your W-2 job, so you might not be able to commit to a target number much higher than that. I also chose it because it impresses many people as a big number, and yet once we break it down, you'll see that it's not that big.

Divided by 12 months, $100,000 a year is $8,333 a month. $8,333 a month divided by four weeks a month is $2,080 a week. $2,080 a week divided by five days a week is $416 a day.

This means that if you want to create $100,000 more a year, you need to create $416 more a day. Figuring out how to find and create $416 a day is the process toward finding your $100,000 Cash Machine.

Now, to some people, $416 seems daunting. The trick is to make that target number less intimidating. In doing this, you will also get a glimpse at changes you might need to make to your business model. A family therapist who charged $150 an hour would need to work three more hours a day to add $416 a day to her revenue. While she was able to work nights or weekends to get those hours, that did not appeal to her. Raising the price of her therapy was not an option either, since she was already in the top range of her market. A silk screener wanted to make $2,080 a week. He sold his shirts for $20 and so needed to sell 104 to reach his target. He sold his shirts at flea markets, and the most he'd ever sold was 50 shirts in a weekend. The weekly revenue target required doubling his sales, not a number he was comfortable achieving. A soccer coach provided clinics for kids' birthday parties. He lived in an affluent town and was able to charge $500 per party, and he had eight parties a month. To reach his monthly target of $8,333 a month, he needed to either double his price or double his output to 16 parties a month. He was not sure he could get there.

And herein lies the challenge of the Cash Machine. The target is $100,000. Changing the target defeats the purpose. The Revenue Model is anchored in the target and built out from there. As I said, unlike other financial analyses, where investors or entrepreneurs calculate what they *can* make, the Revenue Model states what *will* be made. This is not the negotiable part of the equation, it's the constant, which makes the other parts of the equation the variables.

By the Day

The family therapist could not raise her prices, and she couldn't increase her hours. However, these constraints made her creative. In order to make $416 more a day, she thought she should add another service to her business. She designed "morning coffee and confessional" support groups targeted at specific segments of the family. She had Monday for Mothers, Tuesday for Teens, Wednesday for Wives, Thursday for the Mothers-in-Law, and Friday for Fathers. She scheduled these for 90 minutes before her normal hours, which happened to fit in with most people's work and school schedules anyway. She aimed to get nine people per group and charge $50 per person, for a total goal of $450 per day.

Goal	Price	Clients	Actual
$416/day	$50/person	9	$450/day

She would use some of the extra $34 to pay for the coffee and tips to secure the back room in the coffee shop. It took a few months to get the word of mouth going, but once it did, she hit capacity. And though the Friday Fathers group had only four people, the 20 who came for Thursday Mothers-in-Law made up for it. It crossed her mind also to employ other therapists to run ancillary groups or take over hers on an alternating basis.

By the Week

The silk screener wanted to make $2,080 a week, but selling 104 T-shirts a week seemed like a lot to him. He thought about raising his price from $20, but T-shirts at the flea market couldn't sell for much more than that. He then considered a different venue and went to some upscale retailers. This was ruled out because their cut sliced into his profit. A different product might help, he thought. Silkscreen jackets could sell at the flea market for $100 each, and if he sold 20 jackets, his revenue would be $2,000 a week. But the jackets cost him $50, and he didn't like his margins. Another idea came to him. He went to a party planner he knew and presented his personalized T-shirts as a possible premium to include at events. The party planner liked the idea and recommended him to her clients and other party planners. Along with the 50 shirts he sold at the flea market, he sold 54 more a week for each party.

Goal	Price	Clients	Actual
$2,080/week	$20/shirt	104	$2,080/week

He hit his target exactly and made $100,000 a year.

By the Month

The soccer coach wanted to hit $8,333 a month with his soccer clinics. He was already at capacity with eight parties a month for $500 each. He needed to double his volume or his price, but he did not have the time or the market to do that. Again, the constraints forced his creativity. Several parents had told him how impressed they were with the soccer clinics. He'd also sensed that they wished they could participate. There was something missing in town. Many adults wanted to work out, and they also lacked community. It struck the soccer coach that he had other skills, and another market to which he could sell those skills. He'd seen the success of the Marine Corps workouts offered to civilians and modeled that.

The coach created team workouts for adults who wanted another chance at phys ed class. Arranging with the local high school to rent the gym in the winter and the outside fields in the summer, he put ads in the paper evoking the nostalgia of everyone's favorite class and the chance to revisit rope climbing, kickball, gymnastics, and obstacle courses. He also sent flyers to local men's and women's clubs and various organizations in town. The price was $100 a month and he offered his clients ten workouts a month at the relatively low price of $10 each.

Along with his birthday parties, the coach needed only 44 people to sign up.

Goal	Price	Clients	Actual
$8,333/month (incl $4,000 he already made)	$100/person	44	$4,400/month (plus his $4,000 = $8,400)

He continued his marketing efforts, and as demand grew, the coach expanded to other nights a week. He hired retired phys ed teachers and coaches to run those nights. The gym classes helped him exceed his monthly target number of $8,333.

Measuring the Model

The point of the Revenue Model is not just to do the numbers. What makes the Revenue Model such a terrific tool in the Cash Machine is that it actually helps define the business. Because the target is set, the Cash Machine owner must be creative. This type of motivation is particularly helpful in fixing a business or buying a Cash Machine, as it forces the entrepreneur to stretch goals and reach for a better business.

Let's look at running Revenue Models for building a Cash Machine, fixing a business and making it a Cash Machine, and buying a Cash Machine.

Marilyn Stanley wanted her Cash Machine to create $6,000 a month. She knew from her research with Adam that she could charge her clients $75 an hour. She also knew that most Web sites took about 40 hours to develop. This meant that each client would bring in $3,000 a month, so she needed two clients a month to hit her target. This would be 20 hours a week, which she felt she could do herself on nights and weekends. Marilyn also considered that when she wanted to grow the business, she'd have to hire designers.

It's important to note that these targets are *revenue,* not income, so they do not include expenses. If Marilyn were to hire help in order to increase her volume or decrease her own involvement, their wages would come out of that number, and she'd have to change her revenue goals to make more money. Based on Adam's business and her own calculations, Marilyn felt that she had a viable Cash Machine.

Al Cypress wanted to increase his revenue to $300,000 a year. Since one of his major problems was his entity structuring, he would get a bump to his income just from new tax strategies. But Al also thought that he could increase his actual sales with additional revenue streams from his new products. An annual target of $300,000 broke down to $25,000 monthly. With four weeks in a month, this is $6,250 weekly and $1,250 daily for a five-day week. The price he charged for his clinical practice was $100 an hour, and he averaged 30 clients who came twice a month, for a total of $6,000 a month. He was not charging extra for the audio files, and so that was his total monthly revenue, a good $19,000 short of his objective.

Al looked at a few companies that offered self-help audio files and found that they charged as much as $20 a tape. Al's clients, who were generally at the higher end of the socioeconomic scale, were already willing to pay $100 for therapy, and Al thought $20 was a price that they and their peers would pay. He planned to make weekly cycles for each workout regime, and he believed that would bring in an extra $80 a month per client. If half his clients bought the tapes, his monthly revenue would increase by another $1,200. He knew, though, that there were dozens of other athletes interested in his tapes.

Al now needed $17,800 a month. He decided that he would provide a members service, at $100 month, for unlimited access to the audio file products on the Web site. It was this service that he hoped would get him to $17,800, which meant that he needed 178 athletes to sign up for this service of motivational tapes. This type of volume seemed doable in the triathlon race world alone, where hundreds of athletes visited his booth every weekend. He also assumed that many of his clients who were paying $80 a month would pay the extra $20 for unlimited access to the site, and along with his videos and motivational calendars, he thought he could hit the $25,000 monthly goal. Al created a marketing strategy to find and enroll these athletes.

Rosa Brackett wanted a Cash Machine that would create revenue of $250,000 a year and build to a million-dollar business in three to four years. She had the idea that she would buy a local business in town, and she zeroed in on one she liked right away. She knew the owners, she liked the product, and she herself was a customer. The business had sales of $120,000 the year before her analysis. To get the additional $130,000 a year, she needed to increase revenue by $10,833 a month. The owners opened up their books to her, and she also spoke to similar business owners in other areas of the country. They gave her marketing ideas, as well as pricing and volume strategies. The company in which she was interested was averaging $200 per client for service every three months. This was in line with the average pricing from similar companies she researched around the country. By the end of her modeling, Rosa felt that she could get the 15 new clients a month that she needed if she was to hit her first-year goal of $250,000.

Calculating the numbers for this business helped Rosa to better understand the company and its offerings and to consider new strategies. Now she just needed to draw up the plan to see if she did in fact have a viable Cash Machine.

Design the Cash Machine Plan

CHAPTER FIVE

The Plan

Mapping the Best Route

Action Plan						
Seven Weeks to Sales						
Week 1	Week 2	Week 3	Week 4	Week 5	Week 6	Week 7
Skills	Idea	Business Model	Revenue Model	Cash Machine Plan	Team	Marketing and Sales

You've read the fortune cookie: a successful journey begins with a map. That truism applies to business as well. Most entrepreneurs begin their journey with a business plan, a document that maps out the business concept and its strategies. The exercise itself helps the entrepreneur get things going. We all know that if you have to explain something, it helps you to understand it better yourself. Writing the plan down organizes your thoughts and clarifies strategies and tactics. Then, not only does the plan help business owners to think clearly about their concepts and map out the best route, but it also serves as a document to raise money and gather strategic partners.

In my experience, however, a business plan can be a big pain in the neck. I've seen people spend months working on these documents, collecting data and information. The result is a big, fat document of which they are very proud. And then it sits on the shelf. I've also seen people paralyzed by the very process of writing the plan. It can be overwhelming. When Marilyn Stanley was modeling her Cash Machine, she asked Adam Allison if he had a business plan he could share with her. He didn't. This, of course, is not unusual. Most business owners do not have a business plan on their desks. They are too busy running a business. It's the people without a business who have a full business plan on their desk, waiting to be realized.

And there's the challenge. In building, fixing, or buying your Cash Machine, it is important to have a written plan. You'll need it for yourself, and you'll need it to collect your team. But the Cash Machine is created on the job, not at the desk. There's too much work to be done to remain in the theoretical world too long. That's why the Cash Machine Plan is not a traditional business plan. While it's important for you to be prepared and to have your ideas as well thought out as possible in order to map out a direction, refine your strategy, and gather your team, we also want to clear the path to action and get you on your way.

The Cash Machine Plan is one that you can write in one day. If you have difficulty writing, bring in a team member to help get it done. The plan can be as short as one page and should be no longer than three, including the Revenue Model and breakeven analysis stapled to the back. It follows this outline:

I. The Concept
II. The Opportunity
III. The Strategy
IV. The Team and Operations
V. The Financials
VI. Future Pacing
VII. Appendix: Revenue Model and Cash-Flow Analysis

If the writing of the plan gets complicated, that's a good indication that your business idea might be too involved. Keep everything brief and clear. If you need help at this stage, e-mail me at plans@liveoutloud .com, and we'll get you going.

The Concept

Once you've taken the time to determine your skill set and discover an idea with which you can learn to earn and start making money, you are ready to define that idea as a business concept. This is where it's important to note that not every idea, not even every good idea, makes a good business concept. You might want to offer coffee at the workplace, but if everyone there is in the habit of stopping at Starbucks, you're going to have an uphill battle. Since a Cash Machine must get you to sales in seven weeks, you need an idea that generates a business concept that will work right now.

If you don't yet have your concept, you can't begin the Cash Machine Plan. Don't forget: a good concept relies on skills that you already have, so that when you start the business, you are doing something that you know how to do and making money doing it. You shouldn't be learning any skills or learning about any industries. The only thing you should be learning is how to run your own business.

One thing I've found helpful in coming up with my vision for the concept is to ask this question: *What is the experience I want my customer or client to have?*

This angle will help determine the idea. It was one thing for Ray Kroc to decide that he wanted to franchise the McDonald's venue for hamburgers and French fries. But it was another to decide that he wanted people to have a consistent, clean, and quality experience when purchasing this product. The customer experience that you create can, in fact, create the unique selling proposition that you are looking for and can be the factor that makes your Cash Machine both profitable and enduring.

The concept should be one sentence that states the offering and to whom it is being offered. Let's look at ideas that can be ready-to-go Cash Machine concepts in 24 hours. Take a teacher whose skill set was teaching, organization, communication, and encouragement. Her discipline, math, was also part of her skills. This teacher saw that a good Cash Machine idea was to be a tutor. She wrote that her concept was to "create an after-school tutoring service for children ages seven to twelve who need extra help with math." Note how the sentence included a specific idea positioned to a defined target market.

Down the hall from the math teacher was the guidance counselor. Her skill set was counseling, psychology, and communication. She thought a good Cash Machine was to create parenting support groups. She knew that there was a demand not only for advice, but also for community. She wrote that the concept was to "create guidance communities for mothers and fathers of fifth graders on their way to middle school."

The custodian at the school also wanted a Cash Machine. His skills included mechanics, electronics, carpentry, and painting. He believed that there was an opportunity in town to be a handyman for people and wrote that his concept was to "create a fix-it service for homeowners with mechanical, electronic, and carpentry needs."

The librarian had a master's in library sciences, and his skill sets included computers, information technology, database management, communication, and organization. He was also very adept at entertaining children and encouraging their creativity. He thought a good Cash Machine idea, based on his skill set, would be an idea that used that creativity. His concept was to "create an improvisational theater club for parents and their K–2d graders."

In uncovering the concept, you'll also want to start thinking about possible *company names* and *taglines*. The company name should be compelling and stand out, but should also be clear and straightforward. When clients are looking for a car service, they'll most likely look for names that clearly indicate such a service, like Premier Car Service or Drive You Anywhere. If you call the service Four Paws Running, they might get the wrong idea.

The tagline is exactly that, the little tag after the brand. Kleenex had "Don't put a cold in your pocket" when it first came out, and Coca-Cola still uses "the real thing." Names and taglines and slogans are important. These should be clear, catchy, and compelling.

The Opportunity

A concept must either meet an otherwise unmet need or provide for current demand in a unique way. Selling chocolate in Hershey, Pennsylvania, might not be meeting a need. But if your chocolate has a *distinct advantage* or a *unique selling proposition* that will appeal to a significant portion of the market, then you might, in fact, be able to play in Hershey. In this section you will clarify the exact demand that your business will fulfill and how you are positioned to distinctly address that need.

In the example of the math teacher, she realized that there were over a thousand third, fourth, and fifth graders in her town and only one other tutoring service that she could find. That tutoring service did not go directly to the children's homes, and it did not use teachers. There was a need in the market, and, being a math teacher, she had a unique selling proposition.

The guidance counselor believed that there was a very big market opportunity. Her experience included dealing with parents. Though the parents weren't her primary clients, they often demanded much of her time. She realized that no one was meeting that demand. The custodian thought that there was a need for handyman work, but after he began the Cash Machine, he learned that the demand was even greater than he had thought. And as we'll see later, the librarian found a market he didn't even know existed until he put his foot on one strategic path and landed on another.

When considering what it is that your company provides, you will want to brainstorm the *menu of products and services.* This would be a good time to throw everything against the wall and see what sticks. If you're working on an errand service, for example, you would consider grocery shopping and dry cleaning, of course, but you might also add getting the car washed, taking the dog to the vet, waiting for the cable guy, and chauffeuring the kids to activities.

A note on joint ventures: Joint ventures with others can widen the pool of opportunities. Joint ventures are best defined as the pursuit of commerce with one or more partners. In the Cash Machine, we open up the opportunity in the marketplace by creating marketing joint ventures. For example, if you have a valet service, and you know of a housecleaning company, you could refer the housecleaning company to your clients, adding to your menu of products and services. In turn, that company would refer you to its customers, expanding your client base as well. This can be an efficient way to increase your revenue, as long as the other company is reliable and shares your vision of how to treat the customer.

There's also the opportunity to join up with someone who

already has a business and create a Cash Machine as an offshoot of that business. Marilyn Stanley could do this with her Web design company. She could go to her mentor, Adam Allison, and join forces with him to cultivate a new clientele—nonprofit organizations such as governments and hospitals, for example—and use his resources, but her skills, to add those products to his offerings. She could also go to businesses that consult for small businesses and offer to expand their services by creating Web sites for their clients.

Whatever the concept, the signs of a true joint venture are that

- Both parties have skin in the game.
- Two or more skill sets are being combined.
- Both the skill sets and the operations are complementary.
- The resulting product or service offering, though possibly derivative, is ultimately different from what either party would have done alone.
- There is additional revenue to be made, with little cannibalization of any previous business or customer base.

I'm a joint-venture junkie. I've always found joint ventures to be a great way to start a business, expand my learning, build my team, increase my revenue streams, and learn about another industry.

The Cash Machine Plan for a joint venture looks very similar to one for creating or modeling a Cash Machine. Legal contracts would be drawn up immediately, though, so that right off the bat, there is an understanding of who owns what, who runs what, and for how long. Who owns, and has rights to, the client databases, for example, is one of the key issues for joint ventures.

The Market Situation

It's in this section of the plan that you will want to comment on the current market situation. There are three aspects of this to consider.

The first is the *climate*. Describe the general state of the market, the opportunities, and any possible threats. The second is the *competition*. Look at the other companies and players in the marketplace: who they are, what they've done historically, and what they are doing now. The third is the *trends or currents*. This is a short indication of where you think the market is headed and how you will hop on that movement. All of this is helpful in understanding how best to position your particular offering.

The Strategy

The concept defines the strategy, and the strategy clarifies the concept. The strategy is the actual plan of action that will take the business from concept to reality. It is supported by very specific tactics that are employed on a day-to-day basis in each aspect of the business's operations.

The math teacher was going to begin by offering one-on-one sessions to students. Her target audience was children in grades three, four, and five. She would then expand her business by hiring other tutors in other subjects and offering her services in other towns, to reach a wider target audience. With some flyers, word of mouth, and an ad in the local newspaper, this teacher had her Cash Machine idea ready to go in 24 hours. She started tutoring immediately, and her sales began in a few weeks. Her eventual strategy was to expand by hiring other teachers to tutor, in her town and throughout the county.

The guidance counselor's strategy was to target parents of children in the fifth grade and focus only on groups, not on individuals. As a marketing tactic, she put an open letter in the newspaper announcing a time and date for the first free meeting. Dozens of parents showed up. The first meeting was, in effect, a classic marketing tool: sampling, or letting the customer try without buying.

After that meeting, the counselor suggested a quarterly fee, based on the goals of her revenue model. Four out of five of the parents signed up, and she was up and running in her first week. Her growth strategy was to create more parenting groups, and perhaps branch out to the parents of students in lower grades as well.

The custodian began by offering his services for repair work for homeowners in the town in which he worked. He used display ads as an initial marketing strategy and hoped to later rely on word of mouth and referrals. Hiring other handymen was also part of his ongoing strategy. The custodian put up a simple ad at the four local coffee shops and at the gas stations. One of the people who called him was a real estate investor who asked if he'd be willing to help her fix up a home she was flipping. This investor then referred him to her real estate agent, who in turn referred him to other clients. The custodian was on his way to sales. His strategy, and concept, evolved that very first week. He focused more on home renovations for real estate investors who were flipping houses, and he included an expansion strategy to reach out to more Realtors and hire other handymen to do the jobs.

The librarian's initial strategy was to put a print ad in the paper with a reference to his Web site, where people were encouraged to sign up for the improv classes. There was no interest. He decided that his idea was still good, but that kids and their parents might be the wrong market. The librarian changed his concept, his market, and his strategy. He revised the concept to "provide improvisational seminars for corporations to inspire and promote creativity." He chose to market to employees of large corporations. And he developed a strategy to position his product for human resources personnel. The librarian dropped off letters to as many human resources professionals as he could. One company called and scheduled a seminar. He started generating revenue. And more important, he received good word of mouth and referrals.

The Team and Operations

Outlining the team, from management to operations, pushes you to understand what it is you are looking for. Not only will it help you to define the positions you will need to fill, but it will help you think about who should fill them. In this section, it's also important to consider the entity structure and forecasting that you plan to use for this business.

The teacher called a business leader in town to ask if she would be her first mentor. Though this business leader had no experience in education, the teacher felt that she needed business help more than education help. The guidance counselor called a local psychologist to see how he ran his group sessions, and the psychologist came on board as a mentor. The custodian's first mentor was actually one of the real estate agents he met. She gave him a lot of free advice, as well as client referrals. He also asked her boss, who ran the largest real estate firm in the county, to come on board as a mentor, and she agreed. The librarian went right to a human resources professional and got quick advice on how to sell seminars to large corporations. The HR professional became the librarian's first mentor.

As the teams were filled out, accountants, lawyers, bookkeepers, and systems managers became part of these Cash Machines. In the beginning, you may also need to hire consultants. Though an initial cost, consultants can be helpful in getting started.

The teacher needed more tutors, so other teachers became part of her team. She also enlisted principals and guidance counselors and offered them incentives for referrals. The guidance counselor wanted to create more guidance communities, and so she enlisted other guidance counselors. She also initiated strategic partnerships with psychologists and teachers in town who could help spread the word about her company.

The custodian kept his team small, with real estate agencies providing referrals. But then he realized that there were many skilled professionals in town, including other custodians, facilities managers, and even firefighters, who had similar fix-it experience and the spare time to do this kind of work. Once he knew he could expand his team, he increased his marketing efforts, brought in more customers, and pumped up his revenue, but not his time or involvement. The librarian enlisted HR professionals and corporate executives who were interested in creativity, such as those in the branding, packaging, and new product development departments, for his team.

You should also list your support team in this section. If nothing else, it will serve as a reminder to you that you must manage your energy. You need to focus on your highest and best use of time and get others to do the rest.

The Financials

Businesses are run by numbers—there's no getting around that. If a business isn't profitable, it's not a Cash Machine. The point of a Cash Machine is to make money, and the numbers do not lie. In an ongoing business, it's the income or profit and loss statement (P&L), the balance sheet, and the cash-flow statement that present the facts about a company's financial health. But for a start-up business, the numbers tell you if the concept is even viable. There are many approaches to this, but as you've seen, in the Cash Machine, we use the *Revenue Model.* We'll also look at the *breakeven analysis,* which allows you to see how much revenue you need to generate to cover your expenses. The financials section of the Cash Machine Plan should have only a summary of the numbers. The actual financials should be on a separate page, stapled to the back of the plan.

Future Pacing

In the Cash Machine Plan, future pacing is a necessity. A good leader not only maps out the concept and the goal, but sets his or her sights on future benchmarks. The future pacing section of the plan should include a list of projected multiple revenue streams and what products or services will generate these revenue streams. There should also be a summary of the market opportunity for these products or services, target revenue numbers for each, and the strategies and tactics to support these targets.

Building a Cash Machine

Here's what Marilyn Stanley's plan looked like:

Marilyn Stanley's Cash Machine Plan for *Personal Web Design*

The Concept

Personal Web Design provides full-service Web site design and operation for small companies.

The Opportunity

The marketplace is filled with Web site providers, and there seem to be few distinctions between them. Designers in this space provide a full range of services, from technical support to full marketing campaigns, with a trend toward industry specialization. Personal Web Design will emphasize customer service throughout the design process. This will begin with an online questionnaire in which the client shares its intentions, and continue throughout the process with consistent feedback and communication.

The Strategy

(1) Begin with clients referred from Adam and create sample Web sites for prospects to refer to, and (2) use Adam's marketing team to create marketing materials. Initially, these would be blast e-mails. Ads on Web portals, search engines, and classified sites would be a secondary platform for marketing.

The Team and Operations

Marilyn Stanley will be the team leader. Rounding out the team are mentors, including Adam Allison, an accountant, a bookkeeper, an office manager, the marketing team, outsourced Web designers, an intern, and a lawyer. The business will be run from a home office and structured as an LLC.

The Financials

The attached Revenue Model presents the analysis for reaching a target sales goal of $6,000 a month in the first six months. This is based on charging a design fee of $75 an hour and an estimated 40 hours per site development, for a total of $3,000 per site, and working on two sites a month.

Future Pacing

Personal Web Design will offer Web site design and consulting services to small companies throughout the United States and abroad. Revenues will be $10,000 a month within the first 12 months of running the business. Revenue will jump to $20,000 a month in the next 12-month period by marketing to small companies in emerging markets outside of the United States and outsourcing Web work to designers here and abroad.

Fixing a Cash Machine

If the business you own is not a Cash Machine, then you need a Cash Machine Plan to help you figure out how to make it one. Writing down your ideas for fixing the business will help you actually fix it. It will also be a starting point for discussions with your mentors. Let's take Al Cypress as an example. To summarize what we know about him so far:

1. Al was a sports psychologist who had several clients.
2. Al worked many hours and long days.
3. Al's business was not profitable.
4. Al needed to fix his business and turn it into a Cash Machine.

Al's current concept was being a clinical, one-on-one sports psychologist. His new concept was to create motivational audio files and other inspirational products. He knew that there was a large market of athletes, but most of them weren't going to come in for clinical analysis. A new team would be required, including a psychologist or two who could take over the office hours and a Web designer who could help him create a Web site for his podcasts. Al also thought that a marketing mentor might be helpful.

His new plan looked like this:

Al Cypress's Cash Machine Plan for
Gold Medal Motivation

The Concept

Gold Medal Motivation will create and supply products and services to motivate competitive athletes to improve performance. Products include motivational audio files, videos, and inspirational day-by-day desk calendars. Services will include one-on-one therapy sessions as well as group therapy in the form of team support groups.

The Opportunity

The company will target the segment of competitive athletes in southern California who are focused on outdoor sports such as triathlons, volleyball, and water polo. The target audience for the company will be men and women, ages 18–34. The current marketplace is fragmented, with no single brand or company dominating the field. There are no obvious trends toward audio files, although the currents are shifting to a variety of different spiritual and self-actualization offerings. There are psychologists who specialize in sports and motivational speakers whose messages cross over to sports, but there is no large-scale operation offering products and services associated with the expertise of motivating athletes to their highest level of performance. The unique selling proposition of Gold Medal Motivation will be a sequence of specifically staged empowerment messages to get the athlete to the highest possible level of achievement in sports.

The Strategy

Ultimately word of mouth will be the best source of new business. Initial positioning will be to the current base of clients. In addition to their counseling, they will be given a free audio file to listen to during their workouts. They will then be directed to the Web site to purchase the next audio file in their particular series. Other products, such as videos and the inspirational calendar, will also be available on the site. These first clients will be offered the opportunity to become representatives of Gold Medal Motivation, and incentives for the sale and distribution of products and services will be created. The eventual goal is a multilevel-marketing campaign built on word of mouth. Signage and premiums, such as T-shirts and hats, will be sold at sporting events to seed brand recognition.

The Team and Operations

Al Cypress is the team leader. The current team will be expanded to include

- Three well-known athletes, one from each of the sports that Gold Medal Motivation is targeting. These athletes will be brought on board as advisors and spokespersons. They will also be motivated to represent the brand at sporting events and trade shows.
- A mentor in the field of motivational products and services, who will act as a consultant and advisor.
- A professional with experience in multilevel marketing to come on board as a colleague and possible sweat-equity partner.
- A psychologist who can bring some of the one-on-one clients into his or her practice.
- A Web site designer to create the Gold Medal Motivation Web site, with downloadable audio files.
- An entities specialist to structure the companies for each of the products and services.
- A bookkeeper to create and maintain the forecasting and systems for the company or companies.

The operations will be run out of a home office.

The Financials

The current economics of the psychology counseling service will be improved by the new entity structuring, which will allow the company to retain more of its revenue through advantageous tax strategies. The financial objective of the new Cash Machine, and its products and services, is to generate annual revenue of $300,000. This requires revenue of $25,000 a month or $6,250 a week for products and services sold. With an average price of $20 per product and $150 per therapy session, the Revenue Model requires 30 therapy sessions and the sale of 90 products a week. The breakdown of this revenue modeling is attached.

Future Pacing

Going forward, Gold Medal would like to shift the balance of offerings from services to products, so that a larger share of volume and revenue comes from the products available on the Web site. By the end of a 24-month period, Gold Medal Motivation would like to have

- One-on-one and group therapy sessions by at least three outsourced therapists and a dozen motivational products available on the Web site
- National distribution and brand recognition expanding into at least three other sports categories, such as mountain biking, marathons, and cycling
- Monthly revenues of $40,000 by expanding the number of representatives and distributors associated with the brand

Buying a Cash Machine

If you have the financial capacity to acquire a Cash Machine, and you've decided that the fastest way for you to learn entrepreneurship will be to buy a business, you still need a Cash Machine Plan. It would not be wise to buy any business without formulating a plan for that business.

First and foremost, the Cash Machine you buy should be an ongoing business with sales. You will work to increase those sales and/or the profit margins in the seven weeks to sales time period, but you have to find a venture that is already generating cash. It may not be a lot of cash, and there may be plenty of room for improvement, but there should be cash coming in.

When you buy a business, especially if you luck out and find one that's exploding with cash, you may think that the business plan is best left alone. But that's never true. Of course, don't fix a part that's not broken, but every business, like every individual, always has room for improvement.

The concept, for example, may be obvious, but even that can be rethought by a new owner. If you're buying a tooling manufacturer, it might have been running as a status quo tooling manufacturer for years. In the concept section, you might consider adding a precision metalworking division and a consulting operation. The new concept would be a "tooling manufacturer that provides craftsmen with a wide range of products and services."

Each section of the Cash Machine Plan is worth looking at when you are considering how to move your Cash Machine forward. The team is often an area where efficiencies can be made. If the team that is currently in place has been around awhile, you might be able to infuse it with some new energy. Marketing is another area where you can usually add a lot of improvement. If you buy a company that's been selling its product exclusively to retail stores, you might want to look at other channels of distribution, such as the Internet. Operations is often ripe for efficiencies, sometimes within its systems or structures, or maybe with the general layout and product flow.

If you buy your Cash Machine, chances are that you will be bringing investors and bank debt in on the deal. These investors and lenders will be especially interested in the financials. It's here that you'll want to give some thought to how to improve sales or lower expenditures with operating efficiencies.

The business that appealed to Rosa Brackett to purchase was a window-washing company that a friend of her son had started when he was in college. Though the business had expanded from a one-man operation to dozens of employees and hundreds of clients, the owner was now in graduate school and was losing interest in the enterprise. He found it difficult to manage his labor and had no time to build the clientele, yet alone manage the systems. He was way behind on his accounts receivable, and he knew he needed to make a change with the employees if he was going to keep his client base. A larger company had made its way into town, but it was a national chain, and his clients were irrationally loyal. A client herself, as were most of her friends, Rosa thought that this might be a perfect Cash Machine for her.

In acquiring a business, it is important to begin with due diligence, the process of research and investigation that is essential for any investment. As I mentioned, I cover this in my book *The Millionaire Maker's Guide to Wealth Cycle Investing.* Rosa had an advantage in her due diligence in that she was a customer of the business. The perspective of a customer is an excellent one for a prospective buyer because it offers a view of the company that the original entrepreneur doesn't have. Rosa was aware of some problems and opportunities that the boss might not have even known about. Additionally, she knew the owner very well and was comfortable asking him very specific questions. Rosa also knew that he was showing her all of his accounting information and not just highlights.

Her biggest advantage, though, was that she was able to finance the project through the previous owner. Though she knew he wanted to cash out, she also knew that he was willing to wait for a bigger payoff going forward. The operating efficiencies were somewhat obvious to both the buyer and the seller, and so they agreed that she would pay him over three years, with an escalation if the business expanded and the profits increased. Both sides felt that this was a fair deal and a good negotiation that benefited each of them.

While she did her research, Rosa also began her Cash Machine Plan. As you will see, there are a few differences between this plan and one for building or fixing a business. These include the threats portion of the opportunity, an emphasis on the ongoing strengths of the operations, and changes to improve weaknesses.

Rosa Brackett's Cash Machine Plan for *Clear View Window Washing*

The Concept

Clear View Window Washing is a locally owned and operated window-washing company for clients with residential, retail, and commercial properties.

The Opportunity

The window-washing sector in Fairview, North Carolina, is a consolidated marketplace with only two competitors, including Clear View. Clear View's unique selling proposition is its personal approach, availability, and reliability. A distinct advantage is that it is the practice of the organization to hire local teenagers, and these homegrown employees are related to or know a fair share of the market. Threats to the opportunity include the large-scale marketing strategies, systems, and operations of the competitor. The trend in other markets is toward these large-scale, apparently impersonal service providers, and in the event of franchise backlash, Clear View will benefit from its mom-and-pop image.

The Strategy

Current marketing is through display ads in the newspaper and referrals. Additional marketing plans include e-mail blasts and direct mail coupons in bulk mailers. New tactics include a guarantee to customers for a month after each service, annual pricing plans at a discount rate, and refer-a-neighbor incentives.

The Team and Operations

The team is led by Rosa Brackett. The current owner will stay on board as a consultant and advisor. Routine and regular performance reviews for employees will indicate a need for changeover, and new clients will indicate a need to expand the employee base. A bookkeeper will assist with the accounting and systems. There have been no offices, though trucks and equipment are parked, for a fee, at the local parks and recreation commission. A corporate entity for protecting the business and forecasting revenue and expenditures also needs to be established, and an accountant will be hired to help with this task. The revised tax strategies will yield immediate improvements to the bottom line.

The Financials

The numbers show current monthly revenue of $10,000 based on an average of $20 a window for residences and corporate offices and $50 a window for storefronts. The objective is to increase volume by five new clients a month, at an average of $200 a client, to hit a 12-month revenue goal of $22,000 a month.

Future Pacing

Goals going forward include increasing the product offerings to include holiday decorating and gutter cleaning, getting local government contracts with the schools and other municipal businesses, expanding into neighboring towns, and generating monthly revenues of $36,000 by month 24 by expanding into new markets with several product offerings.

Franchises and Multilevel Marketing

Other options for buying a business include franchises and multilevel-marketing (MLM) ventures. Franchises are outlets of business concepts and properties that are licensed from a business owner. MLMs are networks of marketers that create chains of distribution for products and services. They can be good Cash Machines; however, they can also be nightmares. One of the first things you'll notice about franchises and MLMs is that they have a lot of marketing and advertising support targeted not to consumers, but to potential additional owners. This aggressive pursuit of owners should be acknowledged. While there are many reputable franchises out there, there are several that spring up every day that may not have any potential for success.

One of the reasons that a franchise is a good Cash Machine is that franchises are designed to let you learn to earn. They have systems in place, usually developed over several years by experienced professionals, that the franchisee can follow. This allows you to learn in a safe environment, almost a paint by numbers business venture. Many people do not consider owning a franchise to be entrepreneurship because no part of the business was developed, or even improved upon, by the business owner. But that doesn't mean that it can't teach you the skill set of entrepreneurship and the management, marketing, sales, finance, and operations tools you need to run a business. That's a good Cash Machine—if it makes money.

MLMs are another way to learn to earn and make money. These too, though, can be good or bad. There are way too many unsupported pyramid schemes out there that have invaded the territory of MLMs. But true MLMs are not pyramid schemes and can work out very well for wealth builders who have initiative and follow-through. If you have direct experience with the product you are selling—that is, if you are a consumer of the product—and it has benefited you in some way that you can speak about with enthusiasm, then you may do well marketing and selling that product. This is a quick way to learn marketing and selling, and the experience, as with all new businesses, can be exciting or frustrating.

Contrary to popular belief, most MLMs compensate people fairly for what they've done. Unfortunately, there have been several companies that preyed on stay-at-home moms with "in your spare time" messages. But it's called net "work" marketing, not net "sit-on-your-couch" marketing. It takes work, and if you're interested in working hard, you can do very well. Don't forget that the point of a Cash Machine is to find your fastest path to cash. If you think a franchise or an MLM is that fastest path to cash, then it might be the best Cash Machine for you.

Research is your best friend when you are looking for a viable franchise or MLM. A search through the Internet will introduce you to the opportunities out there. Conversations with franchise and MLM operators are very helpful, especially if you find an owner on your own and not through a recommendation from franchise headquarters. Also, you want to understand the difference between a franchise and a license to run a business. Franchises often provide extensive support systems, such as supplies, databases, and advertising. They also tend to ensure exclusivity in your market. Some licenses to operate an outpost of a business may be just that, with no support whatsoever. These possibilities will surface during due diligence, a process that is essential when you are considering a franchise or an MLM as a Cash Machine.

The business plan for a franchise or an MLM may be supplied to you by the company itself. Again, this systematic, done-it-already approach can be a very efficient way to learn business ownership, and the business plans can provide you with a lot of immediate insight. But, because some franchises are better than others, you must keep a critical eye on the opportunity at all times. Mentors who've been there and done that are indispensable.

The Partnering Proposition

As you consider what form your Cash Machine will take, you may discover that the best route, given your skill set and experience, is to join forces with another entrepreneur who has a complementary skill set. This entrepreneur might be building or buying a Cash Machine in which you can become involved, or he or she might already have the Cash Machine and could bring you on board to improve it. If this is someone who is going to drive you crazy, not represent you well to others, act in a way you can't respect or trust, or waste too much time and energy, then this is a bad idea. But if this entrepreneur is someone whom you know you'd enjoy spending several hours a day with, trust, respect, and think you can learn from, even if he or she is also just starting out, partnering with this person is a good idea.

Though the Cash Machine relies on a known skill set to learn the new skills of running a business, you may come to realize that your skill set is not complete enough to create your own Cash Machine. Marilyn may be terrific at Web site design, but perhaps she'd want someone to come in and run all the marketing. She might consider partnering with a marketing executive who is interested in building a new business. This is very different from hiring help. Obviously, the person with whom you partner has to understand the objectives of your Cash Machine and share your drive for success.

As I mentioned earlier, another great way to learn a business is to work for an entrepreneurial venture. Technically, this is not a Cash Machine, unless it makes you more money immediately. But it is a fast way to pick up a lot of good learning. And if you negotiate for equity or stock options as part of the deal, you might walk away with something more than knowledge. Working with an experienced and skillful entrepreneur is more important than the company for which you work. Since a widget is a widget, this business should show you how almost any small business can be run. Though there are lessons that can be learned from watching an entrepreneur run a company into the ground, it's better to use success as a model. Do your homework, and find a good person with a good business to work for.

When you are considering partnering, you should ask for the business plans of the companies that interest you. Not only will these help you learn business plans, but they will give you a map from which to work and enhance your learning. If you are coming into a business as a senior-level partner, you want to be sure that you have a chance to participate in drawing up the business plan so that you can help inform and steer the direction of the venture.

Structures and Systems

Once you have an outline of the plan, whether you're building, fixing, or buying a Cash Machine, you're ready to decide what type of *legal business structure* you're going to have. This is referred to as an *entity.* You will create the entity while completing your Cash Machine Plan.

Every Cash Machine, without exception, must be structured as a legal entity. When you have a Cash Machine, you live and lead a corporate life, which means that all of your assets are held in companies, corporations, trusts, or partnerships for liability protection and tax strategies. In addition to deciding on an entity and setting it up, you need to create a proper accounting system to keep track of your finances, including your revenues and expenditures. This chart of accounts will help you manage a detailed tracking system for all the money coming into and going out of your company—and eventually companies. In addition to structuring your business into a legal entity and setting up a system for forecasting your financials, you'll need to create other accounting, information, marketing, and sales databases and software systems. We'll go over them in the chapter on operations. Your next step is to find the professionals and colleagues who can help you do all this.

Build your team

CHAPTER SIX

Building a Team

Finding Players for Each Position

Action Plan *Seven Weeks to Sales*						
Week 1	Week 2	Week 3	Week 4	Week 5	Week 6	Week 7
Skills	Idea	Business Model	Revenue Model	Cash Machine Plan	Team	Marketing and Sales

The best entrepreneurs are great leaders. And great leaders know how to build great teams. Leaders know enough to understand that they do not need to do everything themselves. There's just not enough time in the day or energy in the bones. Anyone who has succeeded in any endeavor has done so through a great team. Successful politicians have strong political teams. Winning athletes have experts on their bench. And smart businesspeople collect a group of daring doers to help them get it done.

The biggest damper on business creation and growth is an entrepreneur who does not understand the difference between being *in* a business and being *on* a business. Business owners who are *in* their business not only do not see the forest for the trees, but usually try to do everything themselves. Business owners who are *on* their business maintain a birds-eye view of the business and the world around it. And that means they have to have a team.

Good leaders put together great teams by inspiring those around them. People like to have a purpose and a mission, and if they do not have one of their own, it can be equally, if not more, rewarding to join a team that is moving toward a challenging and exciting goal. The best team players, though, are not just team players, but leaders in their own right. They are self-motivated and resourceful, they know what needs to be done, and they are action-oriented. If you find yourself micromanaging your team, then the team is not serving its proper function in your Cash Machine. It's your duty as a leader to find good team players and motivate them through your

- Energy
- Clear vision
- Obvious sequence of steps and achievable goals
- Fair incentives

In your Cash Machine, you will often be both a leader and a team player simultaneously. If you have an experienced professional who has agreed to come on board and manage the daily operations, you may find that the best approach for that part of your business is to follow this person. You may have a Cash Machine that offers a support service, such as bookkeeping or graphic design. This will require you to be a team player for other people's businesses while leading your own. Being both a leader and a team player is not uncommon; in fact, you'll find that many good leaders are good followers.

A working Cash Machine has a cooperative and energized team. We all know the cliché about that one bad apple. That truth is spot on. If someone on the team is not encouraging and supporting and facilitating the vision, that person has to go. There are too many hurdles facing a business; the last thing you need is a roadblock from within. Though it may be difficult, you need to make the decision to cut players sooner rather than later. In most cases, the problem only gets worse if you do not. Attitude can be contagious, and people are capable of spreading good or bad feelings very quickly. Selecting the best people from the start is the best-case scenario, but it often is not possible. If you've made a mistake in hiring, cut and run, and if you can't bear to do such a thing, think of your team. Holding on to a bad apple is not fair to the rest of your team. Similarly, if you're part of a team that smells funny, move on. You are not looking for new best friends here. You are looking for people who can take action. Your energy and efforts are too valuable to waste on working with people you don't enjoy and respect.

Get a Team

Teamwork is a constant theme in the Cash Machine. In order to understand what kind of team you'll need for your Cash Machine, you can rely on a few sources. One is the team of the similar business or organization that you modeled. When you look at the personnel structures across a variety of businesses, you'll see that even though the companies do completely different things, their structures are similar. This falls under "a widget is a widget," because regardless of what different businesses actually do, they usually perform the same way. That's why the model of the Cash Machine works for any company or business idea. And that's why once you learn how to run *a* company, you'll be able to lead almost *any* company.

Part of this same truth is the fact that the organizational and personnel structures of most businesses are very similar. Certainly within a specific industry, or for a specific type of business or type of product, the organizations tend to be similar, all working off the same group of best practices and benchmarks. If you look at the organizational chart of a company similar to yours, you will get a good sense of what you need for your team. If there's no formal chart, you can talk to the owner of a similar business, or you can just look at its operation. The size and type of your business will determine your team. The teams of Cash Machines, like the organizational structures of companies, have many similarities.

Let's look at Marilyn's start-up team as an example.

Owner and president: Marilyn Stanley
Marketing: Marilyn Stanley
Designer: Marilyn Stanley
Bookkeeping: Marilyn Stanley

Well, this might seem like a terrible team. And it is. But when you first start out with your Cash Machine, this may be the best you can do. There is no point in establishing or hiring a team if you have no business. That's why the first members of your team should be those who will give you advice and help steer your ideas and strategy. These are your mentors.

First In: Mentors

Unless you have an initial partner in your Cash Machine, such as a spouse or a friend or colleague, the mentor will be your first team member. You will look for mentors for each stage of your Cash Machine. Some will stay with you throughout the process; others will come and go. For example, before you have an idea, the mentors you approach will be different from those you will seek out after you have the idea.

Your initial mentors should be successful entrepreneurs. There's no reason to have a mentor who isn't successful or who isn't an entrepreneur. You want to learn how to earn, and though you can learn plenty from others' mistakes, successful people make enough mistakes, and they know how to fix those mistakes and do things right. You can't learn how to run a business well from someone who hasn't achieved success in his business. While these mentors will offer their perspective on business in general, they should also help you with idea generation.

Finding a mentor is easier than you think. Seek out some of the business leaders in your town, entrepreneurs whom you respect and admire. There's no reason to target mentors who do not have a reputation for being good people. There are enough successful entrepreneurs to allow you to find nice ones. To meet these people, ask your friends, neighbors, and colleagues if they have any connections. If this doesn't work, make a cold call. If you can't get a call through, write a letter. The letter, though, must be followed up with a phone call. Unsolicited visits are not a good idea. In the worst case, you come off like a stalker. In the best case, you've interrupted someone's schedule, which makes you unwelcome. Most people don't have a lot of time in their schedule to fit in a spontaneous visit. Begin with a letter, an e-mail if you think it will get through, or a phone call. Request a 15-minute meeting. If the person doesn't have time for that, see if she'll let you walk to and from some meetings with her. You might also find a mentor who's not that busy. People who are no longer working are excellent mentors. Often they are looking for something to do, and they might even get excited enough about your business to become involved on a more practical basis.

In Marilyn's case, she was able to find two mentors to come on board.

Owner and president: Marilyn Stanley

Mentors: Adam Allison, a friend of a friend with a successful Web design company, and Susan James, a successful technology executive in town, recently retired

Marketing: Marilyn Stanley

Designer: Marilyn Stanley

Bookkeeping: Marilyn Stanley

Things were improving for Marilyn, and it was only day 3 of her seven weeks to sales. Although Marilyn's team was still mostly herself, she was off to a good start by collecting two mentors. As we mentioned in Chapter 4, "Modeling," Marilyn found her first mentor, Adam Allison, through a friend after "living out loud" with her friend about her Cash Machine idea. Adam had a successful Web firm in Reno, Nevada. His clients were mostly in Nevada, so he was open to helping her start her company in Palo Alto, where she lived. He even suggested that to start, she might want to take on some of the clients he couldn't handle. This was a wonderful boost. Marilyn had not even started her marketing yet, and she already had a chance to secure clients.

Marilyn had also been a longtime admirer of a local technology executive. He was always in the newspapers and was much talked about, but he wasn't easily accessible. Still, Marilyn had a strong feeling that this would be a good match. It took several phone calls, but finally Marilyn got a 15-minute meeting with him. During the meeting, the executive mentioned that he was impressed with Marilyn's persistence, but he pointed out that if it was this hard for them to meet for 15 minutes, he would not be that easy to reach as a mentor. Marilyn knew that he was right, but after all her hard work in tracking him down, she didn't want to leave empty-handed. She asked him for a referral to another mentor. His answer was immediate. As you can imagine, most people don't enjoy saying no to helping someone, and this gave him a chance to do something. He recommended one of his old partners who'd recently retired. He knew that she had more time on her hands, and he thought that she and Marilyn would hit it off. He was right. Susan James was looking for new opportunities. She soon became the second mentor on the Personal Web Design team.

Having been able to get Adam on board quickly, Marilyn got his help in clarifying her skill set and fine-tuning her idea. By the time Susan came on board, the business was already running, and Susan helped with marketing, sales, and operations. Both of these mentors continuously helped Marilyn to solidify her strategies and stay on target.

The Immediate Players

After the skill set suggests an idea and the idea is solidified into a business concept and strategy, the entrepreneur needs to establish the business structures and systems. Unless you can do these things yourself, you'll need an *accountant,* a *lawyer,* and/or an *entities specialist* to help you figure out your entity structure. You'll probably set up something along the lines of a trust, as well as a limited liability company or a subchapter S corporation, the details of which I outline in *The Millionaire Maker,* and which we'll touch on later in this book. Regardless of which type of entity you choose, you will need help setting it up. This might seem like a lot of work at first, but you'll soon realize that it's quite easy. In fact, you can go to your state government's Web site and see the filing papers and instructions for any number of types of companies, partnerships, or corporations. However, I do recommend getting some help with this before moving forward; knowing which entity to pick for your business, as well as which state to file in, can save you a lot of aggravation down the road. As with everything in life, prevention is the best problem solver. The paperwork you have to complete during this stage is worth it. The choice is yours: *you can do paperwork, or you can be poor.*

In addition, you'll need to set up your financial systems. This means you'll need to get a *bookkeeper* on board. Getting your finances into a financial database from the start will save you a lot of time later and pay off big time going forward. As you build more businesses and invest in other assets, these financial databases will make the forecasting of revenues and expenditures into various entities much more efficient. You may also want to get some help creating a database for your clients or customers and for your suppliers and vendors. This means a *database manager* might be added to your team.

As you move into creating your marketing materials, who helps you will depend on your own skills. If you're a good writer with an eye and an ear for the copywriting hook, then you probably don't need a writer on your team. But some people will require help with their marketing strategy from a *copywriter, a graphic designer* or *illustrator,* and maybe, depending on their plan, a *merchandising and promotions specialist.*

With the help of her mentors, Marilyn was able to flesh out her team with immediate players.

Owner and president: Marilyn Stanley
Mentors: Adam Allison, Susan James

Accountant: Sally, Susan's accountant
Bookkeeping: Ted, Sally's bookkeeper
Database Manager: Marilyn Stanley
Marketing: Steve in Reno, a colleague of Adam's
Web Designer(s): Marilyn Stanley

Marilyn set up a limited liability company for her business. She did this through Sally, an accountant whom Susan used. Sally referred her to Ted, a bookkeeper, to help set up a software system to manage the numbers. This would help Marilyn forecast her revenues and expenditures into her entities, another step we'll cover in the chapters ahead.

For now, Marilyn decided to handle the customer database herself, but she did want help with marketing. Though she was on her way to her first clients through Adam, Marilyn needed more clients. In her revenue modeling, Marilyn realized that she'd need at least two clients per month to meet her six-month goal of $6,000 in revenue a month. This meant that she needed to market.

Marilyn had no idea how to market, or even how to find marketing professionals. Her mentors suggested that she look at some of the marketing efforts of her competitors and see if she could use those marketing companies. Since she was unable to reach some of them, and did not click with those she did reach, Marilyn asked Adam if she could talk to his marketing professionals. She liked the work they had done for him and thought they might be efficient at doing it again. Adam agreed to the introduction to his marketing man, Steve.

At this point, however, Adam suggested that he and Marilyn should discuss some financial participation on his part for helping her with the business, referring clients, and sharing his resources. This seemed fair to Marilyn, and they got into the pay or play discussion.

Equity vs. Hire: Pay or Play

As you collect your team, it's inevitable that conversations about payment will come up. Rarely do people, even mentors, do anything for free, nor should they. If there is value in the pursuit for you, there should be value in it for everyone who is helping you. It's not a lot of fun to be a success by yourself, and it's great fun to share your success with as many people as possible. There are probably several ways to pay someone, but I'm going to cover only four here.

One is to *hire* them. This can be done by making them either employees or contractors and usually involves a straight contracted project fee, wage, or salary. This arrangement cannot be random because it affects your systems and structure. A salaried employee may be eligible for certain benefits, such as health care and pensions. There can also be withholding taxes that you have to manage. It's important that you discuss the hiring arrangement with your accountant and/or bookkeeper so that you choose one that is optimal for both you and your employee.

The second way is to offer the person *equity,* or ownership in your company. Though it may seem risky for an individual to take equity (i.e., paper money) rather than salary (i.e., real money), if the company grows, the rewards can be huge. Equity in a start-up company is much sought after by some. Others would rather go for the sure thing in the form of immediate payment. The person's personality, as well as current financial situation, will contribute to the decision on what works.

Though hiring someone often requires immediate payment out of your company's pocket, it's often the best way to bring someone on board. *You should not give away what you can hire.* Equity, although apparently free money at the beginning of the game, can be very expensive as your company grows. On the other hand, sometimes you'd rather choose ownership over salary so that your team has a little skin in the game. When employees and partners are owners, they have a vested interest in doing their very best work to get to your vision.

The third way to pay someone is to give the person *both cash and equity.* This can be the holy grail of payment methods for a partner or employee. Though the person may get paid a little less than she would if she took a straight payment, the chance for an upside is worth the discount.

A fourth way to pay someone is to give a *bonus* based on specific criteria. This is different from an equity position in that the person receives a real cash payout, not just paper profits. In some industries, a bonus can be the bulk of one's compensation, even when combined with salary and/or equity payments.

I currently use a triangle of criteria to determine bonuses at my companies:

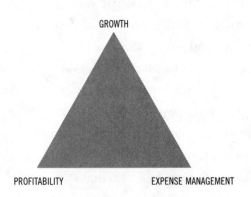

GROWTH

PROFITABILITY   EXPENSE MANAGEMENT

Too many companies create an incentive for managing budgets and keeping expenses down. This kind of move promotes the "stay small" mentality. I've also seen bonuses that were created just for salespeople who want an incentive for generating, well, sales, with no corresponding responsibility for profitability. This Bonus Triangle supports interdepartmental interdependence. Because of the criteria, our accountants have an incentive to come up with ideas for growth that the sales staff can employ, and our sales staff is rewarded if it helps keep the costs of sales down.

Any combination of salary, equity, and bonus works well if it motivates your employees and team members to help the company grow efficiently and effectively.

Mentors and accountants can be very helpful in deciding which ways to compensate members of your team. Usually, each person on the team is paid in a specific way, tailored to that person's experience, personality, and job or position. In the case of Adam, Marilyn and he decided that he would receive a percentage of the fees she received from his clients. He also received a percentage of the fee she paid to his marketing team. Marilyn paid a straight fee or wage to all the rest of the people on her team. At this point, her mentor Susan was the only one who was not being financially compensated.

The Organization

As the business grows, Cash Machine owners may find that they need an organization that is more in line with that of a traditional business. This would include

- Management
- Marketing
- Sales
- Operations
- Finance/Accounting

These positions can be filled by colleagues, professionals, employees, or maybe some interns, or they might be outsourced to vendors. It's possible that you will be bringing some of these skill sets to the game, so you don't need to fill all of these positions.

Sometimes, though, you may want to hire help just to make the company more efficient.

As you'll see in the chapter on expansion, as your company grows, your perspective on hiring will shift. At first, you'll hire what you can afford. But moving forward, you'll anticipate, and hire for, growth. Cash Machines can grow quickly, and it's easy to fall behind. You'll see that you can get stuck if you don't have the right players on board. The people who help you start a company—those wild and independent entrepreneurial spirits—may not be the right people to help you manage it in its maturity. As your company grows, you'll begin to look out a year ahead and hire sooner rather than later.

If Marilyn is doing all of the Web site development herself, there are only so many projects she can do. As the company grows, she may find that she needs to get some help along the lines of a bigger organization.

Owner and president: Marilyn Stanley
Mentors: Adam Allison, Susan James
Accountant: Sally
Bookkeeping: Ted
Office Manager/Systems/Database Manager: Jack
Web Designers: John, Jennifer, and Julie, local graphic and Web designers, hired as contractors; Billy, an intern
Suppliers: Local stores/vendors for office equipment and supplies
Marketing: Steve
Sales: Marilyn, Adam
Lawyer: Stan, a colleague of Susan's

If Marilyn were to lay this out in a traditional organizational chart, it would look like this:

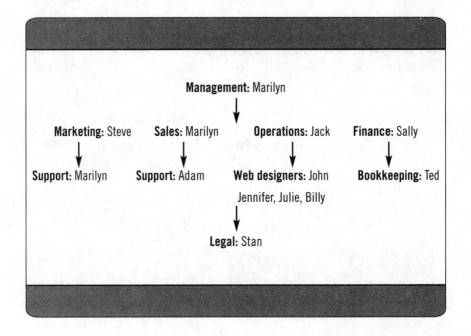

Management: Marilyn

Marketing: Steve   **Sales:** Marilyn   **Operations:** Jack   **Finance:** Sally

Support: Marilyn   **Support:** Adam   **Web designers:** John   **Bookkeeping:** Ted
Jennifer, Julie, Billy

Legal: Stan

Marilyn was still the hub of the wheel, but now she had other team members who were responsible for specific departments. With her office manager, Jack, overseeing the operations of the Web designers, Marilyn could focus on overall strategy and sales.

It's obvious that having an initial team helps create a stronger, more fleshed-out team. Many of Marilyn's team members came from her mentors. Adam helped her get the marketing team. Susan helped her find the accountant, the bookkeeper, and the lawyer. As the work became too much for Marilyn to handle on her own, she hired several Web designers, each on a per-project fee basis. She also found an intern to work for an hourly wage. All these contractors worked from home, so Marilyn's only overhead was the hiring of a full-time office manager and the supplies the manager needed for operations.

Much of the basic team was built by week 6, but Marilyn had started building her team from day 1.

Week 1	Week 2	Week 3	Week 4	Week 5	Week 6	Week 7
Skills	Idea	Business Model	Revenue Model	Cash Machine Plan	Team	Marketing and Sales
Family/ friends	Mentors	Strategic partners (competitors)	Colleagues	Accountant Entities specialist Bookkeeper Lawyer	Marketing specialist	Later: Operations manager Web designers Interns

After she'd reached her sales in seven weeks, the growth of her team would only continue. As Marilyn's team grew, she was able to jump from using the skills she already had a lot and learning a little entrepreneurship, to using less of her known skills and focusing mostly on entrepreneurship. And she made money to boot. That is the wonderful and prosperous learning curve of the Cash Machine.

Growing Constituencies

When you finance your business, you may find that you need investors to give you money or lenders from whom you can borrow money. These people become very much a part of your team. Managing your *investor relations* and your *lenders* is one of the most important skill sets you'll use in building your business. In the beginning, Marilyn was financing her business herself. Her start-up costs were not high, and her main investors were her husband and herself. She did, however, begin a relationship with her local bank.

She set up her accounts with them and took the time to meet one of the small business loan officers in order to establish contact for any potential financing needs going forward.

You may find that as your business grows, you need more of a *sales force* to reach your clients or customers. You might even need a middleman to help you manage the process better. For some Cash Machines, the customer is not the end user. For example, you might have a new product that you're going to sell through department stores. This means that your customer is the store, not the consumer. These stores become a vital part of your team, and your relationship with them must be carefully maintained and nurtured. This might require you to hire a customer relations middleman, such as a *sales representative*. Even if your customer is the end user, you may find it beneficial to reach the many through the few. If that's the case, you will want to hire a specific vendor or similar channel of distribution to get your product or service to these consumers more efficiently. At first, Marilyn needed little in the way of a sales force because Adam was referring clients to her. She'd also achieved the coveted word-of-mouth advertising from her first few clients.

If your Cash Machine requires you to manage your relationship with your community or even spin your customers' perception of you, you may find that another constituency is the media. Many businesses use public relations as part of their marketing strategy. Given that messages through the media can be incredibly effective in selling a product or service, a *PR professional* or media liaison is a valuable team member whom you might want to bring aboard earlier rather than later.

As you can imagine, large corporations have dozens of constituencies that they must manage. A business team can be huge and global, and your Cash Machine may become huge and global one day. The team-building skills you learn now will help you when you get there.

The $400 Solution: Life Support

Your team is not limited only to the business and its various operations and constituencies. In order to build a successful Cash Machine, you may need a little help on the home front, what I call *life support*. Millionaires do not do housework. If you spend 10 hours a week cleaning your house, tending to the garden, and doing errands, that's 10 hours away from your Cash Machine. Most of these jobs can be taken care of by employees for $10 to $20 an hour. Let's say you spend 40 hours a month taking care of your home. That is a whole extra workweek that you can add to your pursuit of wealth for as little as $400 a month. Think about that. Once your Cash Machine is up and running, you could be making $400 a day. That time you spent dusting the curtains or pulling the weeds is much better spent focused on your business. In fact, if you have a Cash Machine and you do your own laundry, you're stealing from yourself. And you can tell your spouse I said so.

Since these team members will be in your home and your personal space, it's important to get reliable references for each person you hire. You can't be remiss in this. I even have a different alarm code for each employee so that I know who is entering and leaving the premises and when. In the beginning, you may not have enough work to give to each of these employees. That's actually a benefit because you can team up with friends and colleagues to hire specific professionals. A personal assistant can work several hours a week for each of three or four different people—which is mutually beneficial to everyone involved. As with all of your employees, in hiring life support, you will need to figure out if you should be paying a salary, an hourly wage, or a specific, contracted project fee. As I've said, these have different tax implications, and you should discuss them with your employee and your accountant.

I have a team to help me at home with errands, housekeeping, and general day-to-day life. I've found that the highest and best use of my energy is to enjoy my family and friends, rather than sitting at my table paying my bills. With my home team in place, I can do that.

Team Dynamics

As with all things in life, businesses change. People change; the operations, the strategy, everything changes as the business grows. As the leader of your business, you need to adapt to these changes. That means staying flexible. The leader of a Cash Machine must anticipate and future pace the possibility of these changes. You may even outgrow your mentors and need to trade up to others. This can be very difficult and uncomfortable, but it is necessary if you, your business, and your wealth are going to continue to grow. Change is inevitable, and it's best to plan ahead for it.

With most of your partnerships, it helps if you always have contracts. Drawing up a piece of paper at the beginning of a relationship may be annoying, but it can save you a lot of aggravation down the road. I always tell my clients, *design your business divorce while you're still in love.* Call it a *pre-entreprenuptial,* if you will. Change sometimes creates fear, and most people aren't particularly rational when they're fearful. If there's an agreement in place, one that already outlines the consequences of the change, then that change is a lot easier. Most experienced people understand the importance of contracts and don't take them personally. When potential team players make the contract stage of the game difficult, it is sometimes indicative of how they will behave going forward.

If you are buying a Cash Machine or fixing the business you have, you are probably all too aware of changes in the team that need to be made. These changes can't be overlooked. Switching bad employees and partners for good ones is one of the most important operating efficiencies you can bring to a business. Though there may be some short-term pain associated with making the decision, you'll probably see the benefits of that change immediately.

As your Cash Machine grows, so will your Wealth Cycle. This means that you will have several assets, including, perhaps, a few Cash Machines. Though you may have a core group of advisors, you will probably have different teams for different parts of your Wealth Cycle. This might seem like a lot of people to manage, but it's just a fact of business and your leadership tools will get stronger as you build your business. The team will also get better. Good teams are easier, not more difficult, to manage. As you generate your wealth, your team will get better, it will take over more of the daily grind, and, over time, you will grow wealthier with less effort.

CASH MACHINE CASE IN POINT

Motivating the Motivator

Even before Al Cypress made the decision to shift the focus of his Cash Machine from one-on-one clinical psychology to motivational audio files, he had issues with his team. Changing the team was not only a good idea but a vital move if Al's business was to survive. And it wasn't just that Al's team consisted only of him and an accountant, although that was something to look at. The bigger issue was that his accountant hadn't been too helpful in structuring entities and protecting the business. When Al suggested to his accountant that he create an entity, the accountant said that he couldn't, that the business was a sole proprietorship. With this structure, Al wasn't getting the benefit of the tax code and the incentives created for small businesses. He was taking home less money than he had made as a salaried employee.

As is typical in these situations, Al went back and forth with the accountant. This type of decision is difficult, and trying everything possible to work it out (i.e., wavering) is common. Finally, Al decided that he needed to trade up. This wasn't easy. The accountant was an old family friend, and Al had some guilt associated with firing him. But this decision led to the first step in getting the new team built. Al walked next door to the salon and wellness spa and asked the owner for his advice. The spa owner explained how he had created an entity that allowed him to take certain tax elections he couldn't take as a sole proprietor. He explained how it worked, and he also referred Al to his own accountant. After an interview with the accountant, Al had two new team members, a mentor and an entities specialist.

This was just the beginning for Al. He continued to build his team. In addition to the entities specialist, he hired a bookkeeper to establish systems to forecast revenues and expenditures. He also hired a psychologist to take over the one-on-one therapy sessions. As Al pursued his better, bigger business, he focused on building an extended team. His next step would be to actually generate revenue from the new product offering, the motivational audio files.

Al Cypress had done his setup work in six days and was ready to go. That might seem fast to you, but if you commit to building, fixing, or buying a Cash Machine, you too can be ready to go fast. Al did it by devoting his first two days to digging into his real *skill set* and brainstorming the *idea* that would best utilize this skill set. As the idea surfaced, he made a phone call or two to find a good *model business* and interviewed the owners. Once he knew what he might be able to do, he chose his target sales number for the next year, plugged it into a *Revenue Model,* and drew up a *Cash Machine Plan* to better understand the strategies that would support a successful pursuit of that target number. During all this, he began the process of gathering his *team* through phone calls, that walk next door to the salon owner, and reaching out to an accountant, a bookkeeper, and a Web site designer whose work he'd seen during the course of his research. Al had taken action. Not only was he gathering information and getting knowledgeable, but he had taken real steps to turn his business into a Cash Machine that would feed his Wealth Cycle.

The Cash Machine is no place for procrastination or perfection. The idea is to use what you know so that you can own and run a business as soon as possible. Marilyn Stanley did this in creating her Cash Machine. She identified her *skill set,* created a viable business *idea* based on those skills, found a business after which she could *model* her idea, tested its potential through *revenue modeling,* drew up a *Cash Machine Plan,* and gathered her *team.* She did not hold involved planning sessions or endless meetings. There was no big business plan document or feasibility study. What she had was a business idea that was ready to open its doors immediately.

Rosa Brackett was also ready to go. Based on her *skill set* of organization, communication, and management, she felt that a good business to acquire would be one that could benefit from her abilities and she *brainstormed the businesses* to consider. In short order, she'd found the company she wanted to acquire, as well as better, bigger businesses after which she could *model* a strategy to make this business better. She ran her *Revenue Model* to make sure the business would be worth her while and then drew up a *Cash Machine Plan* to get to her goal. She also found mentors from the model businesses and worked closely with the previous owner of her business, as well as its current customers, circling the wagons of her *team.* Rosa was careful and purposeful in her research, but she was also eager to get going. It was time to learn to earn and make more money. The operation was already up and running, so she could just jump on the machine and pump the accelerator.

The Cash Machine is all about getting from idea to action quickly so that you can make money and learn to earn as soon as possible. With their plans and teams in place, the time had come for the action. Marilyn, Al, and Rosa were all ready to jump from what they knew to what they didn't know. This meant that Marilyn needed her business to be running, Al needed his new division to get off the ground, and Rosa had to begin to uncover ways to make the business better. What they all needed to do was . . .

> *Market,*
> *market,*
> *market*

CHAPTER SEVEN

Marketing and Sales

Engaging and Enrolling the Customer

Action Plan *Seven Weeks to Sales*						
Week 1	**Week 2**	**Week 3**	**Week 4**	**Week 5**	**Week 6**	**Week 7**
Skills	Idea	Business Model	Revenue Model	Cash Machine Plan	Team	Marketing and Sales

Learn to Earn *The Entrepreneurial Skill Set*				
Management	**Marketing**	**Sales**	**Operations**	**Finance**

Marketing and sales are the vital links that take the owner of a Cash Machine from concept to execution. Obviously, Marilyn, Al, and Rosa had learned a bit already, but most of that learning was in the concept and organizational stages. It was time for them to learn while they earned, and that meant generating revenue. Revenue comes from people buying your product or service. These people find your business through your marketing and sales efforts.

These initial marketing and sales efforts are the last of the start-up steps, and with these efforts, the Cash Machine should be up and running. Once your Cash Machine is on its way, you will delve deeper into the main areas of your business:

- Marketing
- Sales
- Operations
- Finance
- Management

This is the entrepreneurial skill set that you are venturing to learn, and we're going to bridge to here from the action plan with marketing and sales. First, we'll cover guerrilla marketing, which gets initial customers in the door. Then we'll cover long-term marketing and sales strategies, which are part of the entrepreneurial skill set and which you will use to sustain and grow your business.

Engaging the Customer

In order to develop your marketing plan, your Cash Machine team needs to know how you define your business: what you do, how you do it, for whom you do it, and why you do it. Answering these questions will help you discover your *message,* which will be the basis of what you use for all of your marketing materials. My company, Live Out Loud, states that we "make millionaires in three to five years."

Then, once you understand your *target market,* the message is arranged to appeal directly to that specific group. Live Out Loud "educates motivated team players who want to make more money and build sustainable wealth." The message then must fit into the *marketing vehicle.* Our company uses a lot of online advertising, so the message must stand out, be brief, and create a call to action. As the company grows, the message, the target audience, and the marketing vehicle will most likely change too. IBM began as a manufacturer of punch card machines. Today, I don't think most people even know what punch cards are, but, of course, we recognize IBM as a worldwide leader in personal and business technology.

When you begin your Cash Machine, your marketing team will probably be just you—and any good friends or colleagues who are willing to help you out. This is all right. You, using several clever tactics, will be enough to get business in the door and the revenue coming in.

CASH MACHINE CASE IN POINT

Seminar Sampling

Bill, the corporate accountant mentioned in Chapter 4, decided that his marketing message was "strategic tax planning" and that his target audience was "individuals who do their own taxes." His initial marketing vehicle would be flyers and personal connections.

After calling a few independent accountants and modeling his revenue for the personal tax returns, Bill was ready for clients. His Revenue Model committed him to doing at least 20 personal tax returns. He set his marketing plan in place. His gym, where he worked out daily, let him put up posters and flyers, but this yielded no new customers.

Bill asked people if they'd seen the flyers. They said yes. He realized that while he'd managed to create awareness, he had not created an intention to purchase the service. After asking potential customers a few more questions, he found out that it wasn't that his workout buddies were using someone else, it was that they didn't think they needed any help. They were doing their own taxes through a computer program or filing a 1040EZ form.

Bill decided to create a market for his product by educating his friends and acquaintances. He held free "how to save thousands on taxes" seminars at the gym, at his apartment, and even at his favorite bar.

These paid off, and he found his 20 clients.

The seminar sampling case study is an example of good marketing. It's nothing fancy, just simple and clever. Let's break it down and analyze what Bill did. First, he defined his *segment* of the market—people who do their own taxes—and then he zeroed in on a specific *target*—young adults, ages 18 to 34. He *positioned* the product as tax-saving advice for the middle class.

In classic marketing, this is called the STP approach: Segment, Target, Position, This is a good place to start creating a marketing strategy. As with any marketing idea, this can be complicated or simplified. As you can guess, I suggest you keep it simple. The ultimate STP strategy is *niche marketing*. This is the idea of narrowing in on a very specific segment of the market. Often, these segments are small, but because they are so specific, and because the demands of the consumers within them are similar, the market can be penetrated efficiently. Al Cypress's Gold Medal Motivation was pursuing a niche market by going after competitive athletes in competitive sports. Given the large number of consumers on this globe, even the smallest niche can mean big revenue.

What made Bill's marketing strategy smart was the free seminar. *Sampling* has one of the highest conversion rates (i.e., turning potential customers into buyers) of any marketing technique. Sampling should be used only if your product or service works on the assumption "try it, you'll like it." If you can get people to taste/use/see/feel, etc. the product, you can get them to buy it. By educating his consumers, Bill helped them to understand that they did in fact have a need that could be filled by his services.

Sharon, a pharmacist, was aware that there was a large *segment* of the market that was bewildered by medication. She honed in on a specific *target:* seniors, age 62 and over. Then she *positioned* herself as an expert who was able to provide personalized assistance with drug information to individuals and families.

CASH MACHINE CASE IN POINT

Implied Expertise

Sharon was a pharmacist who worked at a large drug chain. She was a salaried employee who was not making as much money as she'd like, and she wanted to create a Wealth Cycle to build her wealth. Because she had no assets, she needed to make more money. She needed a Cash Machine. In addition to her obvious skills of drug awareness, Sharon also had excellent interpersonal skills. Her customers often commented on how good she was at explaining the different drugs and their indications, as well as helping them to make decisions about their drug and insurance plans.

Sharon's plan was to create a Cash Machine that would provide personalized drug and medication consultation at the customer's home. She would organize a customer's medicine cabinet and get it current; explain what drugs the customer had, what could stay, and what had to go; and review the customer's current insurance and drug plan options. Sharon spoke to her employer and explained that she wanted to keep her job, but wanted to run this business outside of its purview, as her own company. She hoped that the store would recommend this service, and she explained to her employer how her business would benefit consumers and be an attractive feature for the store.

That was one of Sharon's first team-building, as well as marketing and sales, efforts, because she needed to bring the store on board as a strategic partner. Her boss agreed with her assessment, and Sharon was on her way. She put a sign for her service in the store window. Not much happened.

Then she had an idea. Sharon wrote up several of the questions that her customers asked most frequently, and answered them. She called it Ask Your Pharmacist and submitted it to the local newspaper as a potential column. The editor liked it and committed to printing the series with a byline, including a reference to her store. After the column ran, Sharon's first customers walked in the door looking for her.

Sharon's marketing strategy is another smart approach, setting oneself up as an expert. People will pay for expertise, especially if it helps them to clarify a complicated situation or area. Drug plans and medication are complicated areas that everyone deals with at some point in their life. By using the newspaper column as a marketing tool, the pharmacist established herself as an expert. She also implied third-party, that is, the newspaper's, endorsement. Oh yeah. This kind of marketing is just oh so good.

The entrepreneurs in these two examples had some hurdles to overcome in their initial marketing. The first, the accountant, needed to educate the market to understand that it needed his service. The second, the pharmacist, needed to establish herself as a trustworthy advisor. There are, however, many times that the first marketing effort requires only that you know how to spread the word.

Let's look at Bob, the administrative assistant I discussed in Chapter 4 when we went over revenue modeling. He created a "personal assistant service to organize finances, maintain filing and databases, and do scheduling." He was going to charge $25 an hour, and he needed three clients who would require four hours of assistance a week. His *segment* of the market was busy people without support systems, specifically small business owners and people who did lots of charity work. He decided to *target* the latter and focused on wealthy individuals. He *positioned* himself as an efficiency and organization specialist for those who have too much to do.

CASH MACHINE CASE IN POINT

See How Flyers Fly

Bob created an entity called The Right Hand Man LLC. Aware of several high-net-worth individuals who not only were overcommitted to the charity circuit, but also congregated in specific areas of town, he decided to target this audience. He knew that these people had a lot of paperwork, errands, and correspondence to keep up with and no time to do it.

Before Bob tried to market to these people, though, he wanted to know what, in fact, was the best way to market to them. He did a little research. Bob asked a few of the executives at his company how they had hired the people who worked in their homes. Personal referrals was the overwhelming response. Bob knew that he needed to get the word of mouth going, but that required clients. He thought that a flyer, properly placed, would be his best vehicle for gathering those first few clients.

A flyer needed to catch the eye quickly, be clear and brief, and inspire the client to call. First, he aimed for a clever hook. He created the header

"Eliminate Every Annoying Little Thing"

He believed that this text would catch the attention of his audience without putting them off. He added another line to narrow in on the offer and drive home the need of which his market should be aware. He wrote: "Imagine you never have to do anything on your to-do list ever again." And then he clarified the offer. He wrote: "Personal Assistant to organize your correspondence, filing, finances, and schedule, $25 an hour. Reliable, responsible, and discreet; confidentiality guaranteed. Many references available upon request." Below this, he put his phone number and e-mail.

The specific areas of town where this group congregated included the country clubs, the spa, and a few local restaurants. Some of the country clubs allowed him to distribute the flyers, but many of the restaurants turned him away. He went to the spa and explained to the owner how he could be helpful in maintaining his clients' regular appointments, as well as recommending spa gift certificates when his clients needed to buy presents. The spa put the flyers on the counter.

Bill, Sharon, and Bob each got customers or clients in the door their first week of business. That's the point of a Cash Machine: to get the business going immediately. Sampling, third-party endorsement, and flyers are three good examples of effective and efficient marketing tools that can be used to get going. Here are some other ideas for getting your business started.

A display ad in the newspaper. If your area has a local newspaper with pervasive readership, this is an efficient means of getting your name out there fast. This is a good idea only if it's not too expensive.

Classified ads in the newspaper. The effectiveness of classified ads depends on your business. If your customers are used to looking in the classifieds for the product or service you're offering, then placing your ad here might be effective. But if your target audience never turns to these pages, this is a waste of money.

Internet sites. While these are becoming more and more effective, and may be catching as many eyeballs as traditional advertising vehicles, there's also a lot of white noise to get through. If you know that your business will appeal to the crowd that goes to a particular site regularly, then this might be a quick way to get customers.

Radio. Radio has become a cheap way to get the word out, but it's become cheap because it's not as pervasive as it used to be. If your target audience is captured by a particular station or a program on a station, this can be an effective way to bring in the initial traffic.

E-mails. E-mail blasts can be very effective and efficient. If you have a good list or can get access to such a list, you can hit a wide range of people very quickly. If you can't purchase or get to a list, sending an e-mail to friends and family just to announce your product or service can also create some buzz for you.

Posters and flyers. If you live in an area where you can put up signs in local stores or town buildings, then posters and flyers are a good way to attract attention.

Parties, seminars, get-togethers. Tupperware knew what it was doing when it started its parties, and many products have copied this approach. If you think your business could benefit from a lecture or a demonstration, arrange a social gathering. Customers are drawn to these types of activities and, inevitably, to your product.

Third-party endorsements. If you can get another business or institution to recommend your offering, you leapfrog the introduction stage of new products and services. Publicity is a terrific vehicle for third-party endorsement. A newspaper article about your business can create a lot of recognition. Getting another business to recommend your services is also very effective. And if you happen to know a local celebrity who's willing to help you out, well that's good too. These marketing efforts usually go hand in hand with building your team.

If your Cash Machine is a joint venture, your partner may already have vehicles for advertising that you can leverage. One of the key assets in any joint venture is the database of existing and potential customers. As you'll see in our chapter on expanding the Cash Machine, databases are highly coveted and can be a worthwhile reason to joint-venture. The use of databases of established companies and organizations is an implied third-party endorsement and an effective marketing vehicle.

These are just some of the quick guerrilla marketing approaches to get those first customers in the door. Let's explore the basics of marketing, how it pervades every aspect of your business, and how you can best use it to sustain and build your Cash Machine.

Marketing 101

The importance of marketing for any business cannot be underestimated. Some would say it's everything. That small intangible "umph" that pulls a product or service up from obscurity and puts it into the hands of millions—that's marketing. Marketing is not sales and sales is not marketing, and anyone who says otherwise is confused. Though they are complementary functions, they are different functions.

Marketing is about targeting people who have a need that you can address and getting them to respond to you. Sales is a way of finalizing that response through a transaction.

In the Cash Machine, we simplify these two functions. Marketing is about engaging the customers or consumers. Sales is about enrolling them. That's it.

It's when people confuse the two functions that things get a little messy. Sequencing, or doing the right thing at the right time, is what makes the marketing-sales partnership work so well. If a consumer is pulled into a conversation about a transaction before she's even learned how the product or service will suit her, she might be put off. If a customer is continuously marketed to when he's ready to seal the deal and go home, he's going to get frustrated. A successful Cash Machine requires both good marketing and good sales strategies, each to be considered specifically and in the right sequence.

From Product to Promotion

We are surrounded by marketing. Like entrepreneurship, it is everywhere: television, radio, the Internet, the newspapers, even right inside our entertainment and news via product placement, mentions, or signage. Marketing means many things to many people, and few people truly understand it. When asked about the marketing of a product or service, most people will refer to the advertising. That is only one part of marketing. The product or service itself, the business concept, is part of the marketing strategy. The way the offering looks, feels, sounds, or tastes are all part of the marketing strategy. How much it costs and when it costs less are also part of marketing, as is the very place that it is offered and sold.

Marketing strategies begin at the idea generation stage, when a concept is created to meet a need, and go on to involve every aspect of the business, including the packaging of the product, the presentation of the service, the pricing, the place of sale, and the promotions. In fact, marketing guru Philip Kotler of Northwestern University is renowned for identifying the main elements or 4Ps of marketing: product, price, place, and promotion; these are the anchors of any marketing strategy.

The marketing strategy is your first great entrepreneurial challenge, and it will be a continuous effort throughout the life of your Cash Machine. I've seen some entrepreneurs have problems because they go-go-go to get the first few customers, but then they stop their efforts, allowing the pipeline of potential sales, and eventually the business, to dry up. Marketing is everything in business. It doesn't matter how wonderful your Cash Machine is if no one knows about it. You could have a great idea, but if you have lousy marketing, you'll be in big trouble. But if you have a lousy idea and great marketing, you could actually be okay, for a little while at least. Since marketing covers so much of the business, it is important to be good at this skill set. If this is not something you've done, the Cash Machine is a great place to learn. You'll learn it through trial and error, modeling good marketing strategies, getting advice from mentors, or bringing a marketing expert onto your team.

CASH MACHINE CASE IN POINT

Marilyn Stanley's Marketing Strategy for Personal Web Design

The product. Web site designs. This is packaged as a full-service design company, providing Web site design and helping customers develop their business proposition and marketing messages.

(continues)

(continued)

> *The price.* The service is competitively priced against other Web
> site design companies, at a price that is manageable for small
> business owners: $75 per hour.
>
> *The place.* The service is offered through the Personal Web
> Design Web site. Communication is via Internet, e-mail, and
> phone.
>
> *The promotion.* This begins with referrals from another Web site
> designer in Nevada. It's sustained through client referrals as
> well as e-mail blasts. Under consideration are postings on
> small business resources Web sites.

The *product* itself is at the core of marketing. The packaging of
that product, how it looks, and how it's presented are all part of the
marketing. The point is to engage the customer. Sometimes engage-
ment occurs because of the font type on the box. Every single aspect
of a product, from design to delivery, is part of the marketing of that
product. If it doesn't engage the customer, it should be reconsidered. This is where you want to emphasize your offering's *unique
selling proposition* or *distinct advantage.* Standing out above the
crowd is easier if you can in fact stand out.

The target audience is also part of your product consideration.
Defining the buyer helps in the development of the product and the
marketing strategy. As the business grows, the concept of the offering may change. It might be improved upon, it might be added to,
or it might be switched out for something else altogether. The product should be under constant surveillance to make sure it can continue to support a profitable Cash Machine.

The *price* of the offering can make or break a marketing strategy,
not to mention the business itself. Businesses constantly use price
promotions to drive traffic to the product or service. Not only must
potential promotions be factored into any equation, but so must the

Revenue Model, costs, and competitors' prices. Pricing is tricky, to say the least. But if you have a good business to model and advice from mentors, you can get to your number quickly.

The *place* is the location where the transaction takes place. Sometimes there are many transactions that need to take place for the product to get from its maker to the end user. A farmer grows corn and sells it to a distributor, who sells it to a wholesaler, who then gets it to the retailers, who then sell it to the consumers. Those are all the places for this product, the corn, to be marketed. Place is also called the "supply and demand chain" or the "channels of distribution." Channels are exactly that: the avenues along which the product must travel to get to the consumer. The shampoo manufacturer sells to its customers, which are the food stores and drugstores. These stores then sell to the consumers. Many channels look just like that: from suppliers to manufacturers to wholesalers to retailers to consumers. Some skip some of those partners; others have more stops and turns along the way.

Understanding the importance of this chain in your marketing strategy is vital to your success. If you've been selling your product in a traditional brick-and-mortar outlet, such as a retail store, you might want to consider adding another channel, such as the Internet. Commercial banks are a good example of this trend toward changing or adding channels.

The *promotion* is the piece of the marketing strategy that is most familiar to people. This includes advertising, merchandising, promotions, and publicity. You need to find the best way to create awareness of the product or service that you are offering. The optimal advertising campaign will deliver a message that is *interesting, distinct, relevant,* and *believable.* As we showed with the examples of quick guerrilla marketing tactics, there are many ways to do this. Most likely, these will change throughout the course of your business's life.

Let's look at how Al fixed his business and created his Cash Machine through marketing.

CASH MACHINE CASE IN POINT

Al Cypress's Marketing Strategy for
Gold Medal Motivation

Previously, Al had marketed his business through the usual means of most psychologists, referrals. He'd also set up a table at various events and connected with a few athletes. This was the extent of his marketing strategy. His new *product,* the audio files, videos, and inspirational day-by-day desk calendars, would be at the center of his new marketing strategy. These products would be bolstered by what he called "intensive motivational sessions" for individuals and teams, which was really just a new label for his therapy practice. The name itself, Gold Medal Motivation, would contribute to a new packaging of the product and underscore an image of working toward being the best. Al would distinguish his product from its competition by creating empowerment messages that were specifically sequenced to push athletes to their best performance time after time.

Al chose a *segment* of the market that included outdoor individual and team fringe sports, such as triathlons, volleyball, and water polo, and *targeted* competitive athletes in these sports. His *positioning* in the industry was to be "the brand that offers intensive motivation to competitive amateur athletes." His therapy sessions were *priced* at $150 an hour, which was comparable to the average for therapy in Los Angeles. Al adjusted team therapy prices into a narrow range close to this. He used $20 as an initial price for his other products, again based on the price he saw for similar products in other industries. The products and services of Gold Medal Motivation would be marketed at athletic events and sold over the Internet, and in the offices of his partner-therapists, making the *places* in his marketing strategy many.

Though Al had only signage in the *promotion* part of his old business, the new marketing plan would include more extensive signage and merchandising, as well as sampling, in the form of free audio files for his current clients. Eventually, the promotion plan would center around personal referrals, using athletes as product representatives, with the objective of creating an organization that modeled a traditional MLM.

In the meantime, though, Al needed to kick off his Cash Machine immediately and bring clients in the door. A *guerrilla marketing plan* was necessary. The first thing Al did was to send out a *blast e-mail* to his current clients and to lists he got from various magazines and athletic organizations involved in the sports he was targeting. He sent a different e-mail for each type of athlete and created a specific subject line for each. To the triathletes he wrote: "Do better in your next triathlon guaranteed." To the volleyball players: "You're not playing your best volleyball until you've . . ." And to the water polo teams he sent an e-mail with the subject line "Your team can win the championships, if you . . ." Al sent out over a thousand e-mails on the first day of his new Cash Machine. The lists were fairly well maintained, and only a small percentage bounced back.

That weekend, Al went to a race in San Diego. These events often have merchandise tents the evenings before and after, and Al set up a *table* at the event with the same declaration: "Do better in your next triathlon guaranteed." *Guarantees* are much like coupons and rebates in that they help to push price-sensitive consumers over the barrier to buy. Generally, this pricing tool costs the business relatively little, because requests for the guarantee or redemption of the coupon are relatively low compared to the number of purchases they prompt. Al had a *"buy today"* promotion at the table that offered two audio files for the price of one. He also captured more names for his e-mail list by creating a *sweepstakes* for a free therapy session.

The next day, Al drove north to Westwood, California, and did the

(continues)

(continued)

same thing at a water polo competition at UCLA. And that night Al scurried to Malibu and set up shop at a volleyball beach party. In order to market, Al had to move it, move it, move it. Once the cash register was ringing with sales, he could focus on a more efficient marketing strategy to generate clients. But to get started, he had to push it hard.

Ramped-up activity like this is very common and necessary during the first weeks of the Cash Machine. Seven weeks to sales doesn't happen without a big push of marketing action.

Rosa Brackett had the same issue. She had a business that was already up and running, but she had to pump up sales right away to meet the goals of her Revenue Model. The previous owner had relied mostly on newspaper ads. Referrals also generated clients for him, but not many. Rosa decided that she needed to ramp up the company's marketing strategy. She dedicated a portion of her funds to this particular effort. This is an important immediate expense to keep in mind when buying a business. The cash requirement for marketing should be added to the cost of acquiring a business so that the money is available to be spent from day 1.

CASH MACHINE CASE IN POINT

Rosa Brackett's Guerrilla Marketing Strategy for Clear View Window Washing

Rosa decided on the following immediate marketing tools:

1. *E-mail blasts.* Thinking that her friends and acquaintances in town would be supportive of her business venture, Rosa sent an e-mail announcing her new business to everyone in her address book, 250 names. The e-mail included a 10 percent off coupon for new and old customers who used the service in the next 60 days. She also created a refer-a-neighbor incentive. She

asked those on her list to send her e-mail to their lists, with a CC to her, suggesting that they use the service. For each name someone sent her that converted to a sale, she would give the person sending the name another 10 percent off, up to 50 percent total. In the meantime, she also captured several new e-mail addresses.

2. *Coupon mailers.* Being receptive to the coupons-in-an-envelope bulk mail herself, Rosa decided to try this for one cycle to see how well it did in creating customers. Potential customers relayed the coupon code, which allowed Rosa to track the effectiveness of this offer.

3. *Guarantee.* Rosa added a "clean windows" guarantee to every single service. Such term guarantees, for example, "We'll redo the work for 30 days after the initial cleaning," are as effective as price guarantees. Though they require money out in the form of wages for the workers and lost opportunity for another job, they create another opportunity for interaction with the client and reinforce the relationship in a way that money-back guarantees do not.

4. *Membership programs.* Rosa wanted to try the idea of an annual pricing plan. She would provide service four times a year, or once a season, at a discount to single services. She decided to call this a membership because she thought that had more appeal than an annual fee. Many of her peers were parents who had children moving back into town and buying homes, and so she also thought she might be able to angle these memberships to her market as gifts to new homeowners.

5. *Refer a neighbor.* In addition to the incentive in the initial mailer, Rosa offered all of her current clients the chance, after every cleaning, to get 10 percent off their next service if they referred a client. If they had an annual membership, she offered them 10 percent off a gift certificate.

These five ideas helped Rosa ramp up her acquired Cash Machine. Not only did they bring in new customers, but they helped her create awareness. Rosa's reliance on *e-mail blasts* supported by a commitment to *build her list* was a very efficient approach to marketing.

Building lists is a quintessential Cash Machine marketing technique, as is creating *lead generation.* Rosa was enlisting the help of her customers to create leads, that is, referrals, to new clients. Eventually, Rosa would create affiliate programs and joint ventures with other companies to leverage their databases and build her client list. You should begin thinking about how to build your lists and generate leads for sales as soon as you start brainstorming your Cash Machine idea.

General Marketing Knowledge

Marketing is valuable only if it brings in sales. That's the goal of any Cash Machine marketing strategy. Your marketing idea might be the most creative thing your friends have ever seen in their entire lives, but unless the concept sells your product or service, it's useless. We've all experienced this conversation:

"Wasn't that a funny commercial?"

"Yeah. What was it for?"

"I don't know, but it sure was funny."

That funny commercial is not a good marketing tool because it does not sell the product. Worse, it might sell the concept of the product, but not create awareness of your brand. If the promotion you create stirs up a need without stirring up the need for your particular product or service, you might drive consumers to the competition. A print ad for a beverage that has fizzy bubbles, dangling ice cubes, and water dripping down the glass is very successful at getting you thirsty. But if the image isn't tied to a brand then the advertiser has allowed you to choose any old drink. Do not create demand without directing that demand. If Rosa Brackett's print ad cried out: "Spring is not spring if you can't see the flowers through that dirty window," she's only telling me to get my windows cleaned. Sometimes the need has to be assumed, and the ad can then position itself to fill the need. Rosa might say: "The point of clean windows is a clear view. Make the call to Clear View today and see what you've been missing." That directs demand.

The following are a few marketing concepts you should know about.

Call to Action

The objective of marketing is to get someone to do something. That's why advertisers often talk about the *call to action*. Good marketers create these calls to action in their advertising, which means that the advertisement makes people take action soon. Examples of this are the "Call this number now for your instant rebate" tags at the end of a commercial. Or "Come in today for a special deal" in a print ad. Or "Bring in your used car or truck this weekend only for great trade-ins" barked out from a radio.

A call to action requires a specific time period in which action is to take place, an incentive for taking the action, and an easy avenue for taking that action. The advertising creates *awareness;* a call to action drives an *intent to purchase.* Sharon, the pharmacist who started the drug information service, wanted to use her advice column to promote a call to action. She put a tag at the bottom of her column suggesting that potential customers "come visit me today for more information on this subject." This call-to-action also drove traffic to her store, which kept her boss supportive of her venture.

Driving Traffic

When marketers talk about driving traffic, they don't mean cars. Traffic represents consumers coming to the point of purchase. You can drive traffic to a retail store, a Web site, an event, or some other location. A TV commercial, for example, works only if it gets the consumer up off the couch and into the store, onto the phone, or visiting the Web site. The call to action should drive traffic. Sharon used her advice column byline, where the retail drugstore's name was mentioned, to drive traffic to the store. Additionally, when readers wrote to her, she mentioned her store and suggested that they come by. This drove traffic to both her business and that of her employer.

The Customer vs. the Consumer

These terms are often confused simply because often they do mean the same thing. But generally, the customer is the next person in the supply and demand chain, and the consumer is the end user. Specifically, a consumer is always a customer, but a customer is not always a consumer. Since marketing happens throughout the channels of distribution, it stands to reason that each part of the channel might need a marketing campaign. Sharon first needed to market to her employer to buy into her idea and still let her keep her job. The store itself would serve as a channel of distribution for Sharon's product, so it was one of her customers.

A customer that is not a consumer is often called the *trade*. There are many companies that market only to the trade. Original equipment manufacturers and suppliers of raw materials, for instance, tend to market only to the trade. Pharmaceutical companies used to be allowed to market only to the trade, that is, doctors and hospitals, until the laws changed and let them loose on consumers. Consumer goods companies market heavily to both the trade and the consumer. Coupons, for example, are a marketing tool used for both the trade and consumers. Though they are used by consumers, the trade likes them because they create value for the consumer, which drives traffic and bolsters the store's image as a retailer that "gets good deals" for its customers. Stores often give preference, by way of price features in their circulars, and in-store displays, to products that offer coupons to their customers. That makes coupons a good marketing tool for a consumer products company to use with both the trade and the consumer.

Reach and Frequency

Advertisers like to use these two terms to quantify the effect of various marketing vehicles. Simply put, you attempt to reach as many customers as you can with as much frequency as possible. Once you've chosen your target audience, you want to penetrate, that is, reach, that market and create awareness, through frequency, for your offering.

Reach × Frequency = GRP. GRPs, or gross rating points, are the extent of the reach times the frequency with which the message is viewed. When your Cash Machine gets to the point where you are going to hire advertisers or use a certain advertising vehicle, get some help in doing the analysis of GRPs. For every different advertising vehicle in every different market, there's often a magic GRP number, not too high and not too low, where you get your best bang for the buck. Going widespread on a message one time will create a big GRP number, because reach will be high. But frequency will be low, and the message will most likely be lost in the white noise or messaging clutter.

Sometimes reach isn't worth the price. Take the current trend toward "narrowcasting" rather than broadcasting. This underscores the idea that it's best to zero in on the right people at the right time, rather than blanket the world with your message. On the other hand, hitting a few people many times may create a high GRP because of the high frequency number, but do little to get you a lot of customers because of the low reach number. Conventional wisdom gives three as the optimal number of times to hit a consumer with your message, and some say that throwing out more frequency than that is overkill. The point is, GRPs are relative and obviously depend on the factors in the equation, not just the sum.

Sharon's advice column in the local newspaper had a good balance of reach and frequency. It reached her target audience of seniors in the town and in some of the neighboring towns as well. It also had the potential to go online and reach many others. The weekly appearance of the column gave her message frequency.

Cost per Thousand (CPM)

This is often used in buying and selling advertising. If you buy something like an e-mail blast, for instance, you'll want to know how many dollars it costs for every thousand people you can reach. Like GRPs, this is a term that advertisers like to throw around, and it should be on your radar. Sharon was getting an excellent CPM, since she was paying nothing to reach thousands of people every week.

The Teamwork to Get from Strategy to Tactics

Your marketing strategy is only as good as the tactics you use to implement it. Either you'll come into the Cash Machine with marketing skills or you won't. If you do have those skills, you'll be able to rely on them to get the Cash Machine going while you learn the rest of the entrepreneurial skill set. If you do not have any experience in marketing, however, you'll need help. Most Cash Machines need a good marketer on the team, and if marketing isn't one of your strengths, you need to hire it. Most likely, you can't do everything on your own anyway, even if you do have marketing skills. In the Cash Machine, it's smart to focus on your strengths and make them stronger, then get the team on your weaknesses. In other words, hire your weaknesses.

The first marketing members of your Cash Machine should be people who can help you create and deliver your message. Again, this might be all you, though you may find some friends or mentors who can refine the message and make it most effective. To varying degrees, members of your Cash Machine marketing team might eventually include

- Copywriters, illustrators, and/or graphic designers
- Mechanical engineers, industrial designers
- Packaging, branding, or identity specialists
- Channels experts, such as retail brokers and representatives
- Advertising, merchandising, and promotions experts
- Publicists and event planners

Of course, many a Cash Machine has operated without any of these team members listed above and most Cash Machines can get off the ground with very few. But it's good to recognize that the marketing role must be filled, even if in the beginning it is you who fills it.

The other half of the marketing team is sales. As we said, it's one thing to bring the customer to the door, but it's another thing to put cash in the machine. Once the customers are engaged, they need to be enrolled.

Sales: Enrolling the Customer

The selling of your vision is best facilitated by enrollment. In marketing, the aim is to create awareness; in sales, the aim is to seal a relationship. The best salespeople buy into the consumer's vision, rather than sell their own. Understanding the goals and objectives of the person to whom you're selling will help you bridge the gap between what that person wants and what you have to offer. The best thing you can do to sell a product or service is to facilitate a decision that the customer will feel good about making. If you enroll the potential customer, you take the traditional perception of sales out of it. The sales process then becomes about helping people make a decision and feel good about the transaction that just took place.

Many people are afraid of sales. This is because they don't want to be seen as pushy. But if you believe in what you are offering, and you believe that it is something that will make the customer's life better, then you are not being pushy, you are being passionate.

Here's the difference:

- In pushy selling, the salesperson talks *to* the consumers and attempts to control the situation. In enrolling, the salesperson talks *with* the consumers. There is an effort to find out what the consumers want and help them find it.
- In pushy selling, the salesperson tries to be the decision maker. In enrolling, the salesperson provides leadership, but lets the customers make their own decisions. Responsibility stays with the customer.
- In pushy selling, the salesperson is driven by making the sale and closing the deal. In enrolling, the salesperson is driven by the relationship and works to make it mutually beneficial for both the buyer and the seller.

Marilyn is giving her customers the opportunity to support their business, Al is helping people reach their potential, and Rosa is providing a quality service. These are all good things, and the owners need to be okay about marketing and selling these products and services. If they aren't, the Cash Machine will not survive.

Your sales skills will be put to the test the day you create your Cash Machine. In order to collect a winning team to help you create your business, you will have to sell your vision effectively. The best leaders are good salespeople who have a level of enthusiasm for their ideas that is contagious. Since you need to believe in yourself and your ideas before anyone else will, it may not surprise you that your psychology will play a big part in how effective you are. Confidence and optimism are two of the more obvious characteristics of a good salesperson.

Good salespeople are also excellent communicators. People who communicate well, with clarity around their vision, tend to be the best at selling themselves and, as a result, their Cash Machines. Every salesperson is, effectively, of course, selling him- or herself. The buyer is enrolling in you. When you start your business, you have to *be* the business.

You Have to Buy It to Sell It—Becoming a Product of the Product

There are two levels of communication. One is *conscious communication.* This includes words, writing, and body movements. The other is *subconscious communication.* This is the feeling, or the vibration, that you send out to the person with whom you are communicating. When you sell, you can say and do all the right things, but if you are feeling something else subconsciously, none of the things you said or did will matter to your customer. You know the cliché: it's not what you say, it's how you say it. The feeling you have beneath the surface is infused into how you say something. Believe it or not, the person to whom you're selling can feel this. People will use their gut, their intuition, to make a decision, and much of that intuition is informed by what you relay with your subconscious communication.

We all know that perception and reality are two different things, and in order for you to be successful in your sales efforts, what the consumer perceives she is getting has to match what she actually gets. It's a bad outcome if someone's perception of your product or service changes after the transaction, because you've just created a nuisance that your company needs to handle. An unhappy customer is time-consuming, drains energy, and is never worth a sale.

Before you can sell anyone else, you first must be sold on yourself. If you believe what you are saying, so will your customer. This is not easy if you do not like or believe in your business. If your Cash Machine makes hamburgers and you're a vegetarian, it's going to be difficult for you to sell your products. Alternatively, when you believe in what you're selling, there's no need for tricks. If you truly believe in yourself and your concept, you can sell the reality. The hard sell, through convincing or manipulation, is never necessary and rarely works. Sales should be a positive and authentic experience for both the buyer and the seller.

Many people are hesitant to sell because they fear rejection. The only way you will experience rejection is if you focus on yourself and your needs. If you focus on the customer and what he needs, there's no rejection. Sales is not about you; sales is about the business relationship.

The Steps to Sales

Sell yourself first. This is where you generate the feeling to enroll people. They can feel it, and they can see it. It's called confidence. Own the product you are selling. You want the clients to feel your credibility and your conviction.

Sell your prospect. Get to know your customers and what they are about. Understand the details and concerns of the people to whom you are selling.

Sell their reality. Show the potential clients or customers where they are and where they can get to. Take away their pain and bring them comfort. This means that you have to know, and then address, their concerns. Similarly, you must understand the exact benefit of your product or service and how it is different from what the competition offers.

The following is where you will spend most of your time:

1. *Engage the prospect.* Get clients involved with a claim or question. I don't recommend telling jokes; those belong in the day of the traveling salesmen hawking vacuum cleaners.
2. *State the truth.* Tell your prospects stories that relate specifically to each person.
3. *State the facts.* Use well-researched information to validate each story.
4. *State the benefits.* Educate clients on what they want.
5. *Link.* Bridge the gap between what clients are looking for—the benefits—and what you have—the solution. Questions are a good way to draw out both the problem and the solution from prospective customers. If they state it, they'll own it.
6. *Offer.* Educate clients on what product or service they need.
7. *Enroll.* Ask for the sale, as well as an opportunity to move the conversation forward.

What Makes Sales Work

Enthusiasm. If you believe in what you are selling, you will be excited about what you are selling. Humor, energy, credibility, logic—these are all going to flow from your enthusiasm, and the prospective client will feel this excitement. Articulate it, own it, deliver it.

Customer service. When you think of customer service, you probably picture that counter at the discount department store with the long line or that too calm person on the other

end of the phone line. That is customer service—too late.
You want to take care of your customers from day 1. In the
Cash Machine, we start customer service as part of the initial
sales process. Successful businesses are built on good relationships, and you need to nurture these relationships
throughout your supply and demand chain. If you take care
of your vendors, they will take care of you. Treating people
well is always a beneficial cycle. Marilyn Stanley started each
transaction by talking through the customer's business
objectives. This made her more than a Web site designer.
Customers saw that she was going to put her thinking cap on
for them and help them achieve their goals.

Know and understand the customer. Understanding the customers' and clients' objections is the path to overcoming
those objections and making the sale. You can't keep selling
if you do not understand the problems. Allow prospective
clients to raise objections and ask questions. Then ask them
questions about their problems and help them define the
context of those problems and to articulate possible solu-
tions. One of the best tools you can use is to find another
customer or client who is very familiar with this problem
and who overcame it through your product or service.

The narrative. Stories sell. People believe stories, and they like
them. When it's applicable, get personal. Use your story about
how your product or service helped you and others. It's always
nice to believe that the experience you're about to give them
will have a nice effect, if not change their lives. There's great
power to influence through experience. Rosa Brackett had the
opportunity to share her story of being a customer who "liked
the company so much" she bought it. That's always a good
story, and it was part of her sales pitch.

But be careful—

Stay focused. The point of the narrative is to bridge the relationship with the customer. Long-winded, emotional stories with too much me, myself, and I put too much of the focus on you and off the customer. Be specific, measurable, and indisputable, and share details of the benefits. The narrative should follow this outline: "Here's what my issue was, here are the things I tried that didn't work, and then I found the answer." The point is to help the potential customer make a more confident decision.

Ignite interest. The senses sell. Consider how you can move others to be excited about what you are offering. If you can create a tangible experience—through touch, smell, taste, sound, or sight—you pull the customer into the opportunity. Sampling is a good marketing technique to get this going. Bill, the accountant who led the free tax-education seminars, ignited interest by showing potential customers exactly how they would benefit from his services.

Put the proposition on the table. Let your customers choose it. Customers will see or hear what they want to. Put out as much information as you can, and make it available, so that it is easy for them to say yes. Jim and Dorothy Stephens started with music lessons, but then realized that kids really wanted to start their own bands. They made their product competitive by creating a series of tryouts and got their customers to choose—in fact, compete—to come to them.

Create the reality. Ask the customers how the product may or may not change their lives. In Al Cypress's business, he might easily ask an athlete: "If you don't use this product, how will your life be different a year from now?"—the implication being that it might not be, whereas Al guarantees that his tapes will, in fact, make people better athletes.

Establish a feel-good environment. Whether the customers buy or don't, it's beneficial to your Cash Machine if they feel that they got value from the seminar, the walk through your store, the sampling of your service, or even the conversation. Even without a yes right off the bat, a productive relationship might build. Sharon, the pharmacist, found herself giving a lot of free advice to the customers in her store. Eventually, several turned into clients.

Drive the outcome. As nice as the conversations with your customers may be, you do have an agenda. You should go into every sales opportunity with an idea of how you'd like to end the meeting. If you go into a situation with a "let's see what happens" attitude, what happens may be less up to you than you want it to be. Always have a goal in mind and steer toward it. While it's important that you stay flexible and listen to the customer's needs, you also want to keep in mind the purposes of your Cash Machine. Though Al could have countless conversations with athletes at every triathlon, he had to keep in mind that his goal was to sell his product or else he wouldn't have a business.

Think their thoughts. Before you sell, you need to understand your customer. That's marketing. Salespeople must market. You might want to talk to people who've bought similar products, or talk to the customers of the companies you're modeling. Find out what they thought before they bought. If you know what made them buy and how they felt before, during, and after they bought, you can infuse that into your own process. Though she had her own buying experience, Rosa did some market research. She talked to customers and learned why they wanted their windows washed, what made them decide to get the service and when, and how they felt after the window washers left. If you can discern the customers' decision process and what was said to them just before they decided to buy, you can use this language for your sales.

The Marketing and Sales Relationship

The Cash Machine will have both marketing and sales. And, most likely, you will be running both of them during that first week. Keeping the two complementary and sequential is what's important. If you have signs all over town declaring the "best facial ever or your money back," then, when the customer does walk in the door, the person at the counter had better know about this guarantee or your marketing will be undermined and you will lose customers.

Sales must have marketing's back. Similarly, marketing mustn't promise more than sales can deliver. We've all seen ads that offered "the best cell phone ever," then walked into the store and seen that the product was not even on the shelf. Then, to add a touch of salt to the wound, the store said that "something almost as good" was available. That is the beginning of a terrible relationship. Sales must seal the promised deal. Marketing promises must be delivered, the benefits of the product must be honest, and the offering has to be available at the price and place it was advertised.

CASH MACHINE CASE IN POINT

Marketing Meets Sales

Bob, the administrative assistant, marketed his Right Hand Man Cash Machine with the promise to "Eliminate Every Annoying Little Thing." A woman read his flyer in the locker room of her country club. She'd just played 18 holes of golf, and when she checked her cell phone, she had 16 messages waiting for her. Overwhelmed, she spotted the flyer on the wall and called the Right Hand Man. They met the next day. She told him that she needed help with her scheduling. That was right up his alley. She told him she also needed help with her correspondence, her filing, and some bookkeeping. Bob nodded, no problem. Then she

(continues)

(continued)

asked him to walk her dog. He balked. That wasn't what his business did. He clarified that he offered services in organizing, filing, finances, and scheduling and showed her the flyer again. She shook her head. "You said every annoying little thing." He was surprised that she thought walking her dog was annoying, but he tried to explain that this was not part of his business. She insisted. He suggested that she talk to someone else, offered to help her find a dog service, and told her to call if she'd like his other services. But he didn't take her on as a client. Sometimes sales is a selection process that helps the business owner stop a bad relationship before it starts. Bob thought this customer might be difficult and did not think she was worth his while.

Bill, the accountant who created the Cash Machine to prepare and execute personal tax returns, marketed his services during his free seminars. He promised potential clients the benefit of retaining more of their income and saving thousands of dollars in taxes. Most of those who attended the seminars didn't hire him on the spot, and Bill didn't push them. He asked only for their phone numbers or e-mail addresses and the chance for a one-on-one conversation to assess their situation. This individual consultation served as a perfect transition from engaging to enrolling. During the conversation, Bill was able to uncover and evaluate their current situation. He asked them to share their thoughts on their job, their salary, and what they hoped to accomplish in the next year and the next five years. Though financial advice and life coaching were not in his skill set, Bill felt that it helped to listen to his clients discuss these issues. It gave him a better idea of who they were and helped him steer his approach. Following these conversations, he drove his outcome. He wanted them as clients, and he asked them for their business. Most of those he had a consultation with ended up using his services.

Betty, the jewelry designer, marketed her Wish Now gem bracelets with a display ad in the local newspaper. It announced that she'd be at the local outdoor market on Saturday and included a line of copy that said, "Come to Table 14 and get a free gift." The friend with whom she was sharing the table had cautioned her that some days it was difficult to get people to stop at the table. Betty hoped that the free gift would help her sell enough bracelets to reach her goal of selling ten at $50 each. The free gift was a gem ring that cost her 10 cents to make, and she made 100 of them.

In the first three hours, she'd given away all of the rings and sold six bracelets. This was a good conversion rate, and she was excited to have done so well before noon. Then Betty realized that she'd run out of the free gifts. Now potential customers arriving at the table would be frustrated. She considered leaving, but that wouldn't keep people from remembering the ad, coming by Table 14, and feeling ripped off. Wishing that she'd written "before noon" on the ad or made more rings didn't help. Betty had created a great marketing concept, but she had left her sales leg of the relay without the baton.

Betty quickly drew up dozens of IOUs for next Saturday's market and made sure to make enough rings the next time. She was also apologetic and honest about her mistake with the potential customers. Through sheer personality, she sold eight more bracelets that afternoon, and gave those customers a discount. Being flexible and candid and reacting positively to the situation are important sales techniques.

In the first few days of marketing and selling your Cash Machine's product or service, you will get a better idea of how these two pieces of the entrepreneurial skill set need to work together. Marketing and sales are part of every business, and there are countless models of good and bad strategies all around. While you are running your business, take the time to model what other businesses are doing. Try different approaches. Use your creativity and that of your team.

The Cash Machine Sales Team

Your sales team will, of course, begin with you. As you build the Cash Machine, the sales team will build.

Marilyn had a good situation in that her mentor, Adam in Nevada, was doing a lot of her marketing, and she just needed to close deals with his referrals. But as she grew her Web design business, she would hire other designers and get them to market and sell.

Al used the sales team as part of his marketing strategy. He enrolled athletes to represent his product and sell it to other athletes in a multilevel marketing network.

Rosa had several marketing tentacles out there and her employees would be a big part of her sales team. This is common in companies. The best businesses get a lot of sales efforts from their employees. If your employees believe in the Cash Machine, and in your vision, they will help you engage and enroll customers.

Your Cash Machine sales team might eventually include

- Employees
- Vendors
- Suppliers
- Reps or brokers
- Professional salespeople

Just as marketing and sales work hand in hand, many of your team members may end up serving both of these functions. Organizing this team and creating systems and structures to support it will get you on your way to learning the operations and finance aspects of the entrepreneurial skill set.

The house for your wealth

CHAPTER EIGHT

Operations and Finance

Systems and Structure

Learn to Earn				
The Entrepreneurial Skill Set				
Management	Marketing	Sales	Operations	Finance

Operations

Operations and finance are important skill sets in your entrepreneurship toolbox. Let's start with operations, the machinery that makes everything go. In a factory, the operations would be the way in which raw material comes in the door, travels through various departments, and makes its way out the door again as a finished product. In most Cash Machines, operations is not that clear-cut. The term *operations* refers to the inner workings, the actual infrastructure, the systems, and the structure of your business. It covers everything that needs to happen to execute your concept. The flow of operations, how the components of the product or service get from nothing to something, can make or break a business. A delay in getting raw materials, a bottleneck in production, a stumbling block in delivery—all of these can make a Cash Machine go under. Similarly, the lack of a proper entity structure or poor database and management system can frustrate and stall a business.

If Marilyn Stanley gathered several clients right off the bat, but couldn't design the Web sites in the time frame required, she just sank her marketing and sales efforts. Al Cypress needed to oversee the production of the audio files, the videotapes, and the calendars and make sure the company was not under- or overproducing. Rosa Brackett had to keep an eye on her organization and make sure that her employees were in sync with the mission of the company.

Operations is the core of the Cash Machine. Your management skills will be put to the test as you try to figure out how to build the actual nuts and bolts of the business. Operations begins as soon as you kick off your Cash Machine and continues throughout its life cycle.

Location and Equipment

Every business has different location needs.

At Personal Web Design, Marilyn didn't need more than an office.

An extra room in her home would do, with perhaps a spot in mind for meetings. It's amazing how coffeehouses and hotel lobbies have become the new conference rooms. As for equipment, she needed a computer, a phone line, and, in Palo Alto, a car to get to any meetings.

For Gold Medal Motivation, Al needed an office, a space for the one-on-one and team therapy sessions, and the use of studio space to make the audio files and videos. Recording equipment needed to be leased or rented with a studio, and he needed a car or a van to get to athletic events.

Rosa's Clear View Window Washing needed an office and a location to park the trucks and keep the equipment. She also considered a space where her employees could convene. She needed to continue to lease or buy more trucks, and to maintain or get new window-washing equipment.

From weeks 1 and 2 of the Cash Machine, when you are considering your skill set and ideas, you should also consider location and equipment. If you are a commercial pilot, but you don't have access to an airplane, the idea of creating a commuter air service won't fly. An idea that depends on a retail location has several variables that need to be factored into the Cash Machine idea. If your town has high rental rates for storefronts with no parking spaces, the retail idea becomes prohibitive.

Location and equipment must both be easily obtainable when you are creating a Cash Machine. When you buy a Cash Machine, the equipment must be reliable, and the physical location, if applicable, should be a big part of your decision. A Laundromat in a high-end neighborhood where most people have their own washing machines is certainly not as optimal as one located near lots of small rental apartments. Likewise, the condition and life stage of the equipment is obviously a major part of acquiring a business like a video arcade or car wash.

The equipment and location of others is important, too. A Web site design company that builds on technology that's not easily accessible to the majority of the market will meet hurdles immediately. Opening an outdoor café next to a smelly cheese factory is also not a good idea. Many problems can be prevented if these issues are considered during the first days of brainstorming. Once a choice is made, modeling the way another company has done it often helps to find the answers quickly.

Operational Flow and Patterns

Sequencing, or doing the right thing at the right time, is put to constant use in operations. Just as it's necessary to have the proper layout of equipment on a factory floor to ensure proper flow, it's vital to make sure that each step in your process is properly ordered to provide the greatest efficiency. This is true no matter what you're doing, even if you're at your computer doing copywriting work. Knowing which client's job to work on when and which part of the work to do at which time can make the difference between a profitable Cash Machine day and too many lost hours. Step back and look at the big picture of your business, and set up the pattern of operations that will make you the most money. Modeling the flow and patterns of another company is a great way to discover the best way to design your operation.

Marilyn needed to keep an eye on how she organized the few hours that she'd set aside from her W-2 job to work on her Cash Machine. A chart of the hours necessary for each client, along with a schematic for deadlines, helped her decide which projects to focus on when.

It benefited Al to consider the flow of his clients through his business. At the time he began improving his business, most of his clients were initially in therapy and then became consumers of the audio files. Given that he wanted to initiate new customer relationships via the audio files, and also hoped to have many clients who used only these files and did not have therapy at all, he reconsidered the pattern of his strategy.

Rosa had a very straightforward equation. Clear View made the most money when more windows were cleaned in fewer hours, with less travel to get there, the minimum usage of supplies, and fewer employees per window cleaned. The design of her operational flow reflected these objectives.

Team and Organization

There's a good reason why human resource professionals are paid fairly well. Hiring and managing employees is some of the toughest stuff you'll do in any business. Equally time-consuming are the relationships with suppliers, vendors, strategic partners, clients, and customers. Managing this aspect of operations is often the cause of many a headache, and as you grow, it only gets more difficult. The worst problem is if you grow without having this aspect of the infrastructure in place. With sales booming and/or more work coming in, it's very difficult to play catch-up in hiring.

The organization needs to be considered when you come up with your Cash Machine idea, and it should be solidified in week 5, when you write out your plan. You should future pace your team so that you know whom you need

1. At the beginning
2. As you get going
3. As you grow

This should keep you slightly ahead of yourself. The organization requires you to dig deeply into your leadership skills and your basic conditioning. The dynamics of a Cash Machine can change from day to day, and if you can't fire that rotten apple, you're going to hinder your chances of success.

Systems

Technology makes a lot more things possible, but even those who have only a home computer know that it also creates a lot of problems. You must get the systems you need in place early. Mentors, colleagues, and friends with technology skill sets will prove very helpful right off the bat. Possible systems you might need include

Accounting programs to track

- The chart of accounts for revenues and expenses
- Assets and liabilities
- Sources and uses of cash
- Inventory
- Accounts payable and receivable

Marketing and sales databases to monitor

- Design and packaging work
- Networking opportunities
- Channels information
- Communications
- Lead generation
- Advertising and solicitation material
- Deal or project status

Information technology for

- Technical support
- Backup systems

Although many businesses require similar infrastructure, the actual systems you require depend on the specifics of your Cash Machine. At first, you may have only a simple spreadsheet to keep track of your cash coming in and going out. That may be fine for the first few weeks, but you'll want to get a bookkeeper or someone with bookkeeping software skills on your team right away. The sooner this information gets organized, the better off you will be. Days move fast when you're running a Cash Machine, and the sooner you have systems in place to handle the inflow of information, the better. Even if it means paying your grandson or your niece $25 to set up your computer, do it.

As you may recall, Marilyn's mentor, Adam, told her that one of his biggest problems was collecting his fees from his clients. An accounting system that charts your accounts payable and receivable will, down the not too distant road, be well worth the time and money it takes to set it up.

Entity Structuring

Entities are the legal structures, such as partnerships and corporations, that help to protect you and your business. The purpose of entities is to take advantage of the government's intention to support entrepreneurship. The U.S. tax code has pages and pages of incentives for business entities. Given the importance of business to our country, it's obvious why entities are rewarded in this way. Yet many business owners do not take advantage of these opportunities.

As I've covered in *The Millionaire Maker* and *The Millionaire Maker's Guide to Wealth Cycle Investing,* the wealthy know the tax code. They structure their lives as corporate lives, so that their businesses and they are protected by entities. This is a nonnegotiable step in sequencing your Cash Machine. You must set up an entity for each of your Cash Machines so that you can retain more income and better feed your Wealth Cycle.

Marilyn Stanley needed to protect her Web design business and to take advantage of tax strategies that would help her retain more of her income. It's this step, by the way, that the sports psychologist,

Al Cypress, most likely skipped in his first business venture, creating one source of his many problems. Marilyn needed to create a company, that is, a legal entity such as a partnership or a corporation, that was legally established and registered with the state.

Again, the creation of entities is a nonnegotiable part of the Cash Machine. If you're going to go to the trouble of earning your money, you should go through (or, better yet, hire someone else to go through) the paperwork of retaining it. You can then use that money to build more businesses and invest in more assets and make more money with a thriving Wealth Cycle.

Many people say, "I want to start my own business." And what I've noticed is that unless they create this business with the proper structures and systems in place, they're not going to make any money. Take Al Cypress. He had his own business, yet he was not making any money. A Cash Machine is not just a business. It is a properly structured business entity that supports your strategy to generate and sustain wealth—million-dollar wealth.

An entities specialist or an accountant who understands the objectives of your small business and won't try to talk you out of this type of structure will be one of the first members of your team. There is a rundown of various entities, including options for limited liability companies, partnerships, and corporations such as the popular subchapter S, on many legal and government Web sites, as well as at www.liveoutloud.com.

There are several important factors to consider when choosing the entity that's right for you, including your current situation and your objectives, not to mention the type of product or service you're offering, the type of industry or sector it's in, and the area or state in which you're offering it. There are also many choices, including the type of company and the state in which you choose to incorporate, which does not have to be the state in which you are doing business.

Ask a mentor or an executive at a company that you are modeling what type of entity or entities he or she uses. The experiences of others in legal issues like this are interesting and helpful. However, what is right for someone else may not be right for you, so it is important that you get expert advice on your specific situation. This is one of those areas where you can do more harm than good if you make a bad choice.

You'll also want to plan for the organization of your entire Wealth Cycle, which will include many different assets, such as investments and other businesses. Many wealth builders include the establishment of trusts in their entity planning to further protect and organize their money. The structuring of these entities will change and grow as your wealth grows. Entities are most effective with proper *forecasting*, which requires getting your feet wet in finance.

Finance

We've made this point throughout the book: numbers drive business. If you're not comfortable with numbers, you need to get comfortable with them quickly. The good news is that numbers are not that big a deal. Really, it's true. The purpose of numbers is to create a common language that all business owners and investors can understand, and once you learn this language, you will find it much easier to communicate.

Eventually, when your Cash Machine is up and running, you'll want to create financial statements to help you keep an eye on your business. The following are the traditional financial statements for a business:

1. *Income statement.* This statement is often called the profit and loss statement, or the P&L. This is where revenue and expenses are accounted for, with the remainder for each quarter and the year listed as a profit or a loss.

2. *Balance sheet.* This statement keeps track of the assets and liabilities of the company. The value of all of the assets is balanced by either debt or equity.

3. *Cash flow statement.* The sources and uses of cash, or the actual cash flowing into and out of the business, are tracked from day 1. In the development stage, cash flow is often negative. As it's calculated daily, weekly, or monthly, though, cash in will grow bigger than cash out, and the business will be on its way.

A bookkeeper will keep track of all of your finances. This is one of those tasks that most entrepreneurs choose to hire someone to perform. It's just too time-consuming for most business owners. Your time will be better spent on marketing and management. However, this does not excuse you from watching the numbers. You are still in charge of the details, even if you are overseeing them. Financial responsibility and accountability always fall back on you, the leader of the company.

As the business begins, these statements can be a bit tedious to create, and few small businesses do so in the all-out way that corporations do, or that you eventually will do. You may find it hard to get a bookkeeper or financial advisor, with the result that you'll be doing much of the numbers work yourself. Even if you find someone, you will want to work alongside him. Either way, the traditional approach to financials can be a bit of a hurdle to your progress. That is why, in the Cash Machine, we take our own approach to financials with the Revenue Model. But first, we have to clarify your Financial Baseline.

Financial Baseline: Laying the Foundation

The first rule of finance in the Wealth Cycle is "thou shalt not commingle." This is so important that I'll say it again: "thou shalt not commingle." What this means is that you cannot, you simply cannot, have your personal finances and your business finances in the same books. It's not fair to the IRS, it's not fair to a potential buyer of your business, and it's not fair to you. If you want to send a big old red flag to Uncle Sam, then all you need to do is mix and match your personal and business numbers.

Getting your personal numbers in order is one of the first steps of the Wealth Cycle. It's called the Financial Baseline. It may take you a few days to do this, but it is a vital step in your Wealth Cycle process and a necessary precursor to the Cash Machine. It will allow you to create the Cash Machine financials and to better understand which part of your life goes where. As your wealth builds, you will have several Cash Machines and investment entities, and you will need to keep separate financials for each. Though it may seem more difficult at first, this division of income and expenditures, as well as assets and liabilities, will make your life a lot easier down the road.

My first McGraw-Hill book, *The Millionaire Maker,* has an entire chapter on the Financial Baseline, and it is well worth your time to spend a few evenings, or one weekend day, setting this up. It mostly involves reorganizing your files and putting your accounting into a software program. The results are financials that look like this:

Revenue	Expenditures
Assets	Liabilities

You will have these four squares for your personal life and for each of your businesses. They are simple and straightforward, and they will keep your life and businesses moving forward to support your wealth.

Once your personal finances are set, you can create the financials for your first Cash Machine. This has to be done in a software program. Your manual check-writing system must go away. Everything has to be electronic, because you are going to want to do things with the push of a button.

You'll come to see that in your Cash Machine, those top squares, the Revenue and Expenditures, which are similar to the P&L statement, will be your new best friend. With them, you will be able to identify the *dials of your company* and know where to turn up the heat and where to lower it, depending on what the numbers tell you.

The P&L consists of all your revenue and all your expenditures. When you start your Cash Machine, many of your personal expenses, or portions of those expenses, will move into the business. These might include, for example, your car payments, or parts of them, if you use your car to get to and from meetings and other business-related activities; some insurance; equipment; supplies; and portions of your rent.

By creating a monthly P&L for your Cash Machine, you can see where you've accelerated or decreased your revenues and expenses. The P&L is a real indicator of what's happening in your business. By creating a chart of accounts for revenues and expenses, you can quickly identify how well your company is doing and how healthy your company is. A chart of accounts is just a categorization or labeling of items so that you can divide revenue and expenses into very specific categories to ensure that you are taking proper tax deductions. It also helps you keep an eye on how the different parts of the business are performing. Your accounting system will tell you where you are overspending and underproducing, and this will help you get more sophisticated. The P&L is a great tool to gauge what is going on in your company. As one of my coaches likes to say, it helps you to see *where you are achieving and where you are bleeding.*

The balance sheet is also important. Keeping track of your assets and liabilities is essential, especially in asset-based businesses such as real estate or anything with heavy equipment or large amounts of nonperishable inventory. In a service or support business with no tangible assets, the balance sheet will be more about keeping track of your cash, intellectual property, debt, and equity.

Keeping your personal life and your business life clean and separate will also help you in your exit strategy. When and if it is time to move on from your Cash Machine, you will have the detailed numbers to back up your asking price for this asset.

Financials for Creating a Business

The *Revenue Model* will be the basis for all of your accounting and financials, without hindering the fast pace of Cash Machine progress. Years ago, I developed this approach to keep things simple while still including all of the analysis necessary to stay on track. The Revenue Model sets specific, doable monthly goals that drive action and accountability. The bonus is that this analysis also highlights the discrepancies between what you want to have happen and what is happening and gives you a way to spot trouble areas quickly.

Earlier in the book, in the section on modeling another business, we summarized the Revenue Model. You pick the target revenue you want to achieve and calculate the volume of the product or service necessary to achieve that target. In the initial models, we showed a fairly simple calculation. To get to this summary, though, we need to build the exact numbers that get us there. As you'll see, the numbers go from general to detailed very quickly.

In doing a Revenue Model, there are three spreadsheets you need to create. The first is the quarterly and annual projected and actual revenue.

Quarterly and Annual Projected and Actual Revenue

Product:

Price:

Year 1	Quantity		Gross Revenue	
	Forecast	Actual	Forecast	Actual
Month 1				
Month 2				
Month 3				
Total 1st Quarter				
Month 4				
Month 5				
Month 6				
Total 2d Quarter				
Month 7				
Month 8				
Month 9				
Total 3d Quarter				
Month 10				
Month 11				
Month 12				
Total 4th Quarter				
Total Year 1				

This is similar to the summary we did in that you look at the product or service to determine how much you can sell it for, how many you can sell, and what the total sales, or gross revenue, will be. The calculation is done every month, and the projected numbers are compared with the actual. This measuring of forecast and actual quantity, and its corresponding revenue, every month will give you the much-needed signposts of progress.

Getting to projected numbers, that is, your sales every month, is the first step in Revenue Model. The frustration you're going to encounter is that you may feel like you're just guessing. Well, you are. And that's okay. This is the best way to start. The objective is to project the amount of dollars for each product or income source every month.

To pick these numbers, you are going to want to build to your eventual goal. For example, if your objective is $240,000 of annual revenue, your monthly goal is $20,000. Let's say you want to get to that goal by year 2. The way to get to $20,000 a month is to *begin at the end.* Put that number 12 months out, and then work backward, lowering the monthly gross revenue to a number that gets more and more accessible. In this case, let's say that the doable number is $5,000 a month.

Time Frame	Gross Revenue
Month 12	$20,000
Month 11	$18,500
Month 10	$17,000
Month 9	$15,000
Month 8	$13,000
Month 7	$11,500
Month 6	$10,000
Month 5	$ 9,000
Month 4	$ 8,000
Month 3	$ 7,000
Month 2	$ 6,000
Month 1	$ 5,000

Contrary to logical assumptions about growth—which would lead you to think that the percentage change in numbers should increase over time—the increase may be faster or slower in the beginning, depending on your product or service. I've seen start-ups that have exponential growth immediately, but soon taper off. And I've seen other businesses that take quite a while to ramp up but then zoom. Like everything in life, it depends.

Each of these numbers goes into each of the months in the first spreadsheet as *forecast*. Then, when the month ends, you will fill in the true numbers realized by your business as your *actual*. In this way, you will slowly get historical data and knowledge. This information will directly reflect how well you've marketed your product and the reality of the demand out there, that is, what people need.

The biggest mistake I've seen in revenue modeling is that too many people are scared to guess. "How do I know?" they wonder. Well, you don't. But you've got to start somewhere, so just do it. If you truly can't figure it out, go back to the model company and let it be your guiding light. There were many times, with each of my Cash Machines, that I had to go back to the model company. And not just once in a while. I've gone back a number of times during the life cycle of this or that company. Seven or eight months in, if something is not working, I go back. There is some reason why the model company is making money and you are not, and that is the answer you want to discover.

It's very important that you do not get fixated on numbers. Prepare the Revenue Model in this way and then be open to what's possible. Do not get stuck in your plan. You analyst-personalities out there will have a hard time with this, but you've got to get over that. With revenue modeling, you have to have fixed plans *and* be dynamic at the same time; that's just how it has to be.

Additionally, you may find that as the year goes on, not every product idea and revenue stream in your plan will work. That's all right. In year 1, just go for the one or two revenue-generating ideas that will make your Cash Machine work. Then, in the next year, add more. By doing this, you may find your niche. There is always a good chance that you will not be able to execute all of your ideas. Ideas always outnumber capacity. Just service the niche you discover, or the products that create the best cash flow for your Wealth Cycle, and grow your business that way. For a bird's-eye view of these numbers, see the spreadsheet below.

90-Day and 12-Month Summary of Volume and Sales

Product:

Price:

	Quantity		Gross Revenue	
	Forecast	**Actual**	**Forecast**	**Actual**
1st quarter				
2^{d} quarter				
3rd quarter				
4th quarter				
Total 1st Year				
1st quarter				
2^{d} quarter				
3rd quarter				
4th quarter				
Total 2^{d} Year				

This general summary is done for each product or service. As you can see, by listing the quantity and revenue for each quarter, you can get a quick look at how well your Cash Machine is progressing.

Along with your revenue, you need to account for your expenses. The long list of expenses listed on the left side of the table below means that this is where the details come into play. These items are only some of the expenses that you might have. I've chosen ones that are somewhat universal, such as Internet access, banking fees, legal fees, and entity formation, but each business has its particular expenses as well. Many of your personal expenses may find their way into the business, and they should. If 80 percent of the time you spend on the Internet is for your Cash Machine, then that portion should be listed in the expenditures for the Cash

Quarterly Projected and Actual Expenses

	Month 1		Month 2		Month 3		First Quarter	
	Forecast	Actual	Forecast	Actual	Forecast	Actual	Forecast	Actual
Internet access								
Web hosting								
Advertising								
Banking fees								
Merchant account								
Legal								
CPA								
Web design								
Business writing								
Entity formation								
Business license fees								
Computer support								
Photography								
Stationery								
Shipping								

	Month 1		Month 2		Month 3		First Quarter	
	Forecast	Actual	Forecast	Actual	Forecast	Actual	Forecast	Actual
Postage								
Computer hardware								
Printing/copying								
Office supplies								
Telephone								
Office equipment								
Software								
Travel								
Hotel								
Flights								
Meals								
Mileage								
Car rental								
Transportation								
Professional development								
Total								

Machine. In addition, once you have several companies set up as part of your entire Wealth Cycle, those expenditures will be divided by the revenues they support. Your car might be used for your two Cash Machines, your investments, and your personal life, and the cost of that car will be divided up, based on the percentages it is used for each. This may seem like a lot of work to manage, but once the systems are in place, it becomes a push of a button every month.

As with the revenue numbers, both projected and actual expenses are given for each quarter and for the year. The expenses will match up directly with revenue so that you can see, again, what is the best use of your time and money. If a certain expense—let's say salaries, for example—is overwhelming your capacity for revenue, then that number needs to be reconsidered.

Breakeven

Every Cash Machine needs to run a breakeven analysis. The breakeven tells you when you will stop losing money and begin making money. This is very helpful in identifying your negative gap, which is the amount of money you will need in order to get the business going before the business is living off its own dime.

Every business requires cash out to start. And few businesses have cash coming in on day 1. In most cases where you are building a Cash Machine, and in many cases where you are fixing a broken business to make it a Cash Machine or buying a Cash Machine, there will probably be a lot more outflow than inflow. Potential investors may ask, "What's your burn rate?" The burn rate is the amount of cash you use monthly to get going, before you make a profit. The day your revenues and expenses are the same is when you hit breakeven. See the example of a breakeven analysis below.

Breakeven Analysis								
Month:	1	2	3	4	5	6	7	8
Units/clients								
Price per unit/client								
Total sales ($)								
Fixed expenses (for example) • Salaries • Rent • Utilities* • Insurance • Taxes • Marketing*								

Month:	1	2	3	4	5	6	7	8
Variable expenses (per unit × units sold) (for example) • Material • Packaging • Wages								
Total expenses (fixed + variable)								
Total sales–Total expenses								

*In some businesses, the utilities and marketing may in fact be tied directly to the volume of goods sold. In those cases, these portions would be allocated as variable costs.

This is one of the first analyses you should do. Like the Revenue Model, it takes some guesswork. You will need to create sales projections and expense estimates for each month. Once you've done your research, determined the prices that others are charging for similar services, estimated the sales volume you can create as you penetrate the market, and modeled potential expenses off of others in the industry, you can come up with some rough numbers.

It's important to note that some costs will never occur again, that is, they are nonrecurring charges. These charges, such as the purchase of equipment, will be part of your development stage. In addition, there will be two types of expenses every month, your fixed costs and your variable costs. Fixed costs are the monthly charges that will be the same every month. Variable costs vary with the volume of sales you do and are usually tied directly to the cost of goods sold. Industry trade magazines should be able to give you a lot of this information. Average expenses and other relevant metrics will help you determine your estimates. Mentors and other advisors should also be helpful with these numbers.

The Financials of the Wealth Cycle

Forecasting revenue and expenditures is an important part of the entire Wealth Cycle. Forecasting provides the means to support tax strategies and also to focus on directing money into a Corporate Wealth Account, for more investing opportunities and toward debt service and management.

Each company in your Wealth Cycle should have a *Corporate Wealth Account.* It serves a purpose similar to that of the personal Wealth Account, into which the wealth builder makes a monthly priority payment for investments. Likewise, the Corporate Wealth Account is a special holding account in the Cash Machine for which a portion of revenue is earmarked every month. This priority payment is used to invest in other assets to support the Wealth Cycle objective of creating multiple streams of income.

Another important financial consideration for your Cash Machine is *debt management.* As you probably know, there is both good debt and bad debt, and your Cash Machine should have only the good and none of the bad. Good debt is borrowed money, usually at a low interest rate (somewhere at or around the prime interest rate), that is used to build the Cash Machine and/or create more assets. Good debt is used with the hope that the assets will make more money than the cost of the debt. Bad debt is high-interest borrowing, like credit card debt, that is used for one-time or perishable items that don't really serve the purposes of the Cash Machine. It's your responsibility to manage your debt and find strategies for the use of good debt. No debt at all might seem interesting, but at times, it's not that helpful. Using inexpensive money to make more money is leverage, and it's a smart use of funds. Good debt is managed and adjusted to get the best rates. Bad debt is managed through scheduled, accelerated payments until it disappears.

Let's do the numbers for creating Marilyn Stanley's company.

Revenue

As we've seen, Marilyn's Revenue Model was calculated as follows:

Goal	Rate	Hours	Clients
$6,000/month	$75/hour	20 hours/week	2/month × 40 hours each

In order to reach these numbers, Marilyn would need to work nights and weekends, putting in, on average, an extra three hours every day on her Cash Machine. If she wanted to expand her business or spend less time on the actual work, she would need to hire help, which would be an additional expenditure.

Expenditures

For now, the expenditures needed to support this revenue were:

Computer. Two years old and paid for. This was an expenditure that she could forgo because she was using equipment that she already had. Going forward, if Marilyn needed another computer, the cost would be real dollars out, but it would also create a depreciation expense for her business.

Office furniture. For now, Marilyn was going to use furniture from her home.

Entity structure. Marilyn paid $500 to an entity specialist to establish a limited liability company, Personal Web Designs LLC.

New software. A few new graphic design programs would help Marilyn be more efficient. These cost her $600.

Rent. The space in her home would now be a deductible expense, but it represented no real cash out.

Phone. Again, a portion of the Stanley phone bill would now be listed as an expenditure in Marilyn's financials.

Internet service. Same as phone.

Marketing. The fee for the referrals from Adam Allison in Nevada would go here, and Marilyn would pay for the e-mail blasts and postings on small business resource Web sites. She expected this to cost $100 a month.

Again, some of the expenses are fixed costs, while others are variable costs. Fixed costs do not move with sales, while variable costs are tied directly to sales and can change with the volume of business. There are also nonrecurring costs in the development stage that most likely will not be repeated. These large expenditures are more likely to be one-time, up-front charges such as the computer, office equipment, and any large assets. Monthly expenditures, such as cost of goods sold, are variable costs, and these are the expenditures that eventually can be played with so as to increase margins.

The basic *Ground Floor—Getting Feet Wet Scenario* for Marilyn was to round up two clients a month. While she may hit her goal of $6,000 of revenue, she will also have the start-up time and cost to deal with. Working backward, she might strive for only $1,000 a month to start and build up to $6,000. Or, alternatively, if Marilyn found this goal too easy, she could jump her goal up to $12,000 a month.

Operating Efficiencies

In fixing a business to make it a Cash Machine or buying a Cash Machine, the financials are similar. You will begin with a Revenue Model, name your target numbers, and schedule out your projections. In these cases, you will be working off of ongoing revenues and expenditures. While that sometimes makes things easier, you also have to be on your toes. Sometimes the numbers are not quite right and various threats or weaknesses, such as underfunded pension plans or past-due liabilities, are lingering. Sometimes these threats can be turned into opportunities, or weaknesses into strengths. And as most seasoned business owners know, some weaknesses, such as operating inefficiencies, are the best thing to uncover in a newly acquired Cash Machine.

CASH MACHINE CASE IN POINT

Washing Up Operations

When Rosa Brackett acquired her window-washing Cash Machine, she noticed that not much thought had gone into operations. The previous owner had kept the list of clients and the payment information in a school notebook. He also had made appointments for clients on a random, first-come, first-serve basis, with no thought to the most efficient way to schedule their services. There was no office, he used his personal phone for calls, and the trucks were parked for a fee at the parks commission. This was an opportunity. Rosa could assess these deficiencies and make better choices.

The first thing she did was systematize the *accounting*. She hired a bookkeeper, who put all of the accounting into a software program. An *entities specialist* was paid to consult on, and set up, an entity. After considering the business and Rosa's entity options, they decided to establish a limited liability company. The bookkeeper created a chart of accounts that listed all the revenues, expenditures, assets, and liabilities of the company. She made a *forecast* of these for the company, projecting what she thought it might spend and listing what it actually did spend. Rosa already could see that with the expenditures she was deducting from revenue, she would retain almost twice as much profit as the previous owner had. This was a huge operating efficiency, and all she had done was structure a legal

(continues)

(continued)

entity and set up a software system. The bookkeeper also set up e-mail invoices and a system to *communicate* regularly with customers to collect accounts receivable. With this alone, she shortened the period of accounts receivable from 60 days to 30.

Next, Rosa computerized the *customer database*. Not only did this help her to keep track of her clients, but she could see what services they used and when. She set up a marketing program to send them specific e-mail promotions based on their usage patterns.

By systemizing the accounts and establishing the proper entity, Rosa was able to protect her business, as well as support her tax strategies. By forecasting revenue and expenditures Rosa retained more of her income. This boosted the bottom line immediately. The systemization of the finances for forecasting also helped Rosa to see, and then improve, the areas of the organization that were underperforming.

Though perhaps not as sexy as marketing and sales, operations and finance are the main engine of any Cash Machine. Maintaining these systems and the organization of the business is essential to its growth.

Valuation: The Finances of Buying a Company

If you buy a Cash Machine, you need to do a valuation in order to determine that you are paying a fair price for that business. I strongly suggest that you get the help of mentors and other industry professionals in conducting your due diligence and valuation. Additionally, take a look at *The Millionaire Maker's Guide to Wealth Cycle Investing*, which I released with McGraw-Hill in the fall of 2006. There you will find several simple summaries to help you get started on basic vocabulary and concepts.

Ask anyone on Wall Street and they will tell you that valuation is a little bit objective and a whole lot subjective. Within each industry, there are very specific due diligence checklists. Call a mentor, an accountant, or an attorney in the industry in which your Cash Machine competes, get him or her on your team, get access to the due diligence checklist, and start asking the questions.

Generally speaking and for example, you'll want to look at historical sales and project future sales based on volume and prices. You'll want to look at assets, including inventory, equipment, and goodwill. Goodwill includes intangible assets such as the name and reputation of the company and any intellectual property, such as trademarks and copyrights, from which the company benefits. You'll need to look out for hidden costs of the operations and detect numbers that aren't even there, like certain expenses the previous owner may not have recorded.

When you research your potential acquisition, you will need to ask for all of the financials, tax returns, any letters of intent or contracts, and sales agreements, among other things. Basically, buying a Cash Machine requires a thorough combing through of everything you can get out of the previous owner. Two words: due diligence.

Once you get the numbers, you need to do the analysis to determine the proper price to pay for your Cash Machine. Simply put, the price of the company is whatever the seller is willing to take and the buyer is willing to pay. You can try different techniques to get to this number, but one of the most common is comparable multiples. If similar companies in the industry are selling at 10 times earnings, then you can apply that same multiple, 10, to the earnings of your potential business, and the result is the price of that business. There is also the discounted cash flow analysis, which puts a present value on the future annual cash flow you will receive. Another way to buy companies is to just pay for the assets, often called balance sheet or book value. This relies on a good look at the left side of the balance sheet. Though I have summarized it here, valuation is no small thing. Determining the value of your potential acquisition requires in-depth investigation and careful analysis of the numbers. It's best done with the help of mentors who've done it before, industry peers, lawyers, and accountants. In other words, a team.

Accelerating your wealth

CHAPTER NINE

Accelerating the Machine

Expansion and Exit Strategies

Without growth, operations stall. The Cash Machine must grow. Once the business is up and running, it is important that you revisit the action plan and seven weeks to sales, as well as the entrepreneurial skill set, to feed business development. You will do this throughout the life cycle of your business. As the growth occurs, you'll add more money to your Wealth Cycle, spend less time on the details of your business, and begin to evaluate the future of your business, either through continued growth or through realizing some value from the Cash Machine, much like any asset or investment you want to liquidate. This is when things get really exciting.

Doubling or Tripling Revenues

Hitting your target number is good. Most likely, the day your monthly number is the same as your projected goal, you will be excited, even thrilled. But I'll bet that by that time you'll be so addicted to coming up with new ideas and new strategies that you'll keep going way past that target. Way, way, way past. A mentor of mine once told me that you've only just begun when your annual salary becomes your monthly income. I couldn't believe that could be true—until it happened within the first year of my Wealth Cycle. Now I've leapt past those numbers many times over.

From Top Line to Bottom Line

Reaching the goal beyond the goal means continuously increasing the numbers. This requires looking at your Cash Machine from top to bottom. One focus is on increasing sales. This can be done in several ways:

1. *Increase the number of new customers or clients.* This can be done only if you have enough capacity. Marilyn Stanley's infrastructure may not be able to support this increase in volume, while Al Cypress's can. Marilyn will have to hire more people and build out her organization of Web designers, techies, and consultants. Once Al had produced his motivational podcasts, he put them on his Web site. Al's infrastructure was indifferent to the volume. Increasing the number of new customers requires a corresponding increase in marketing and sales, as well as, for some businesses, ramped up systems and operations.

2. *Increase the number of repeat customers.* This is a good strategy for companies with a limited capacity, such as a laser hair removal center. Since there are only so many machines, technicians, and rooms within a particular facility, each customer is taking up the place of another customer. A new cus-

tomer and a repeat customer fill the same seat, but the marketing costs of creating primary demand are higher than those for retention. Retention marketing programs can include loyalty programs, such as points for visits that lead to discounts. Cash Machine owners need to check the return cycle for each customer. This was a strategy that benefited Rosa Brackett's window-washing company.

3. *Increase multiple transactions.* If a spa customer comes in frequently for massages, but never gets a pedicure or hair styling, there is an opportunity to sell that consumer other products or services at the time of purchase. Similarly, most of the successful online flower companies now sell balloons, cookies, and other gifts. Selling offshoots or flanker products is a great way to increase sales. Bundling products and offering value-added promotions are good marketing strategies. Marilyn Stanley created growth by offering not only Web site designs, but also small business consulting, copywriting, and merchandise that carried designs and logos.

4. *Team market through joint ventures.* There may be only so far that your company can go on its own. Team marketing, or joint-venturing with a host or database, is a great way to increase sales. The partner in this agreement must match your wants and needs with a solution, and vice versa. For example, you may need new customers, and hence a database. Your host, who has a database, may need new products and maybe even a few more marketing techniques, both of which you have. This creates a win-win relationship. By cross-marketing, and sometimes sharing the profits or a percentage of sales, both players in a joint venture benefit. The important thing to remember is that the guy with the biggest database is king. If that's you, negotiate the use of that database wisely.

Businesses joint-venture with other businesses all the time, and as your Cash Machine grows, this strategy may be the best one for you. There was an ice cream vendor in a resort town with a thriving storefront and delivery business. A promotions and premiums specialist joint-ventured with him to create specific products promoting the brand, including T-shirts and hats. They then sold these in retail stores. Another joint venture involved an artist who made high-end, low-volume furniture. She combined with a retired retail buyer. They created a new business by adding low-end, high-volume product lines to her ongoing business and selling them through department store chains. An educator created a joint venture with a company that sold flowers and balloons online. She created a new company off of theirs to market and sell care packages to summer camps, boarding schools, and colleges.

5. *Expand channels of distribution.* Place, the third P of the 4Ps, can make sales zoom. If Betty, the jewelry designer, could market and sell her Wish Now gem bracelets through Wal-Mart instead of at the local outdoor market, that would send her sales zooming. Getting certain channels of distribution, such as catalogs, Internet sites, events, and stores, can spark the fire of your Cash Machine overnight. Finding the buyers or other contacts for each of these channels and targeting your sales pitch to them may be worth all of your marketing and sales dollars and efforts. There's no reason to sell to the many if you can sell to the one who will sell to the many for you. Begin by writing a letter, sending a package of information or the product itself, presenting at the company's offices if that's appropriate, or going to a buyer's event if one is available. Another approach to channels is to find model companies or mentors who have successfully sold to that channel and get advice. They may even call their contacts for you.

6. *Increase your marketing dollars to build marketing strategies.*

Initially, your marketing is most likely to consist of word of mouth and referrals. If you have a good product or service, referrals are easy to cultivate and continue. However, you cannot rely on them for real growth. There comes a certain point in the life cycle of a business when you need to know how to increase your marketing dollars at the right time. Not all at the same time, but at the right time. I've seen Cash Machine owners try to drive direct mail hard or push the Web by putting a lot of money into SEOs (search engine optimizers), pay per click, or automatic e-mail programs, only to find that they don't have a message that pops past the white noise of these arenas. While these options may be available to you, you shouldn't necessarily use them unless they are the right thing for your product and your target audience—and your infrastructure. It is ridiculous to pay for any of these marketing vehicles in the beginning if you can't handle the volume.

7. *Increase infrastructure.* The organization, the sales machine, and the workforce all need to be in place so that you can support increased demand. The worst thing you can do is create the want and not provide for it. Getting the right team at the right time is important. At first, most people overhire. Then, going forward, they underhire. It's a funny, tricky business, that hiring. The most difficult part is the fact that the swashbuckling, jack-of-all-trades, boundaryless team players who get you going will most likely need to be replaced by specialists who know one department or skill set and know it well. I began my company with a handful of energetic, brilliant brains who did everything from strategic planning to taking out the garbage. Now I have specific departments, information technology, sophisticated systems, and human resources. We even have an employee handbook. Previously, I found that once I got one area of my business fixed, another would have a total breakdown. All cylinders

were never firing at once, so I just circled around, fixing one and moving on to another. Part of accelerating my Cash Machine was hiring for growth and getting ahead of myself, so that I wasn't always falling behind. Now the company's growing exponentially, and we finally have the right people in the right jobs doing the right things to keep us surviving and thriving.

8. *Seed development and support execution.* Ideas are cheap; getting them executed is priceless. As you accelerate your Cash Machine and pursue sales, you will want to put money and time into research and development to keep those ideas coming. You'll also want to continue to cultivate all of your distribution and marketing efforts to give those ideas a place to go.

While you are looking at ways to increase sales, you also need to look at your operations. This will support your drive for bigger sales and also increase efficiency, which in turn increases profitability. By looking at the operations, you can see where the Cash Machine is achieving and where it is bleeding. This means pushing the bottom up. Basically, you are looking to

1. Uncover and improve the weakest links.
2. Uncover and eliminate the stalled, stuck in the mud parts of the business.
3. Shore up the leadership and discover where it is present or absent.
4. Stay on your business, not in your business.
5. Ensure that teamwork is in fact working.
6. Determine where integrity is showing up and where it is not.

Continuously monitoring from the top down and from the bottom up is important to the growth and acceleration of your Cash Machine.

Leveraging What You Learned to Earn

Other ways to increase sales and profitability require you to revisit your action plan and entrepreneurial skill set.

Action Plan						
Skills	Idea	Business Model	Revenue Model	Cash Machine Plan	Team	Marketing and Sales

Skills

As your Cash Machine starts to take off, various aspects of your skill set will shine, but others will falter. With each task and each pursuit, you will recognize different strengths and weaknesses. For example, you may have thought that you were into operations, but your time is better spent working on marketing strategies. Or you may have thought that you were weak in numbers, but you find keeping your own books to be quite exhilarating, and you want to save your funds to hire someone to do sales. The best thing about a Cash Machine is that it is yours, which means that you can do the tasks you want to do.

Marilyn Stanley realized that although she was good at Web design, marketing her services and managing an outsourced workforce was a higher and better use of her time. Al Cypress improved his business by focusing on product development and joint-ventured with other therapists to run the clinical side of his business. Rosa Brackett was surprised to see that, although she had thought that her organizational and management skills would help her improve the window-washing business, she had a flair for marketing, and she was able to increase sales with several clever promotions.

Ideas

The Cash Machine begins with a good business idea. That idea will be at the root of getting to sales as quickly as possible. As time goes on, you may change the idea—as Marilyn did when she decided to court small business owners instead of individuals. There is also the possibility that other ideas will spill out from your core idea, creating additional streams of revenue, like the motivational merchandise that Al came up with.

Keep your mind open to the opportunities in the marketplace, and also to the thoughts and insights of your team. Employees and strategic partners often have a perspective that you might not, and profitable opportunities may surface in ongoing brainstorming sessions. I'm constantly approached to develop new product ideas, or buy businesses, or create joint ventures, and I'm always ready for the bullet point sale from anyone who wants to give it a shot. As Rosa Brackett built the window-washing business, she realized that there was a real need for gutter cleaning and holiday decoration. She considered adding these services to her menu of products.

Business Model

As your Cash Machine grows, you may have to look around for new models. The best-case scenario is that your first model is the bigger, better version of what you hope to be and that you can follow its course of action. In most cases, though, your Cash Machine will grow in its own specific way. You will have to continuously revise your strategy and find mentors and models that can help you branch out from your original plan.

Revenue Model

Ah, yes, I know; you kind of hoped that this was a one-shot deal. The surprise, though, will be that you will find yourself revenue modeling in your free time and by your own desire. "What if we added this product?" will be a constant refrain in your brain. Outsourcing to Web designers and joint-venturing with other businesses prompted Marilyn Stanley to see if she could support a Revenue Model at $20,000 a month. She worked it backward and saw that she might be able to get there as soon as her second year of business.

I had a client who created a personal shopping service. She was constantly joint-venturing with retailers in various sectors, such as clothing, jewelry, and wine, and adjusting her Revenue Model accordingly. When that happens to you, it will be a happy day.

Cash Machine Plan

The concept of your business should stay on course, but inevitably, new opportunities in the marketplace will come to your attention, and you'll want to examine the possibility of exploiting these opportunities. Similarly, certain threats might surface, and you may have to revise your strategy. As you make these changes, your team, operations, financials, and future pacing will also change. This Cash Machine is a dynamic process, and your plan should be updated regularly. Al rewrote the Gold Medal Motivation plan several times as he moved away from a clinical practice to provide audiocasts.

Team

It is unlikely that the people with whom you begin will be enough of a team for your growing Cash Machine. Most of the time, you will be expanding your team. You may add strategic partners with whom you are going to joint-venture or hire more professionals to carry out certain tasks. In some cases, the entire team may change. As the business grows, the responsibilities may become too much for some people.

The first Web designers Marilyn contracted with were too slow. She had to upend the roster and start over. Al saw an opportunity to infiltrate more athletic events and doubled his sales force, enrolling professional athletes from several new sports. Rosa realized that college students were sometimes unreliable and that she needed to bring an on-site supervisor on board for the window-cleaning business.

Expanding, changing, and trading up personnel are all part of the requirements of leading a good team. If the bookkeeper isn't on top of the forecasting, your database manager isn't recording new marketing leads, or your lawyer isn't writing up the proper contracts, you will need to communicate better with these players or make some changes.

Marketing and Sales

Each time you try something new, you might want to just run it up the flagpole and see who salutes. An entire marketing strategy built on the 4Ps for every new idea could keep you from moving forward at the pace the Cash Machine requires. Test it, try it, go-go-go. If it works, you can always make the pretty brochure later.

When Al made his tapes, he used an inexpensive little recording device. The audiocasts were not the least bit high-tech, nor the packaging clever. He threw each audio idea on the Web site as soon as he made it, and if it sold, it sold. If it didn't, he pulled it off. Sometimes the tape was fine and the only improvement required was to design the product selection box better or rename the audiocast to make it more compelling. Most of the time, Al was grateful that he didn't spend too much time or money on an idea until he was sure it worked. It wasn't until he moved into selling CDs or saw that the podcasts were hugely popular that he improved the product. And then he re-recorded and created new packaging for those motivational sessions that had already been proven on the Web site.

The Entrepreneurial Skill Set

The skills you bring to the business help you get started and make money immediately. The goal, though, of course, is to learn a new skill set—the how-to-run-a-business skill set, or what we've been calling the entrepreneurial skill set. From day 1, you will see these skills start to improve. Some you will excel at and pursue more vigorously. Others will be trouble spots for you, and you will look to hire help for those weaknesses. Either way, you will certainly know what it is you need to know to run a business. Sometimes just knowing what it is that you don't know is enough to keep you on top of your growth.

Entrepreneurial Skill Set				
Management	Marketing	Sales	Operations	Finance

Management

This skill set leads the game. If you can understand how to lead your Cash Machine and what it takes to get from where you are to where you want to be, you will have a successful business and create wealth. How to sequence the right steps at the right time and future pace the business to get to your goals should become clearer as you write out your plan, execute strategies, and then go back to your plan. For some people, this skill set takes hold immediately. For others, it remains elusive. Either way is all right. If you don't have the skill set, you hire it. As you grow, it will be easier for you to find the best management for your business.

Your *conditioning* and psychology will play a big part in how well you manage your business. Sometimes, growth is in the mind. I've found that capacity is blocked until it expands. There is always a capacity blockage; people set a goal, get to it, and then think that's that. I've seen clients set a revenue goal of $220,000, get to it, and then sit there for the next two years. They just can't get any higher. Their paradigm has hit a hurdle, and they can't get past it. Not only do they need to look at the company and see what can be done to improve it, but they need to change their thinking.

Pricing structure, the volume of clients, and the types of transactions are all part of the growth equation, and the Cash Machine owner can look for a gap in these. This will help spur growth. But the Cash Machine owner also has to *believe* that more growth, great growth, is possible.

Sales and Marketing

Increasing or improving the sales and marketing efforts is always time well spent. Marilyn Stanley was initially relying on referrals from Adam Allison, but in order to grow, she needed to start advertising her products and services.

Sometimes the Cash Machine owner is generating enough leads, but not making enough sales. A woman I worked with owned a spa, where she did laser hair removal, Botox, and microdermabrasion. Her revenue was $30,000 a month. That's a big number, but it was below her expenses. She had a problem that she needed to find and fix. She felt that she was generating leads with the potential to bring in $7,000 more a month. Every time a client walked in the door, he stayed. But not all of her leads were walking in the door.

Soon enough, we found the problem. While her phone was ringing off the hook, the person answering the phone wasn't getting the sale. The receptionist had no idea that it was her role to pull the leads in for the spa experience. Easy fix. The Cash Machine owner retrained the receptionist and explained that the outcome of every inquiry should be a visit to the spa, and soon the leads turned to sales. We also discovered that the most profitable products were in the back of the spa, not at the counter. Place, as you may recall, is a key part of the marketing strategy. She put these products in front, where the customers could see them. Obviously, there are many parts of the marketing and sales strategy that can help increase revenues.

And, as we've said, *joint venturing* is another way to grow your Cash Machine. In addition to going directly to her target market to create clients, Marilyn could joint-venture with another business to benefit from its client base. Marilyn went to a CPA in town and suggested that they joint-venture. The idea was that she could help him expand the menu of his products and services by offering his clients, mostly small businesses, Web design services. For her part, Marilyn would increase her client base. The key to joint ventures, as I've said, is making sure that the business you partner with is reliable and shares your view of how to treat customers.

Operations and Finance

Changes in the organization and the systems will always be part of growing. You will probably find that you need to hire help. By outsourcing the Web design work to designers at an hourly wage, Marilyn could increase her revenue. More interesting for her, though, was that this could decrease the amount of time she actually needed to work *in* the business, and increase the amount of time she spent *on* the business. That was the right direction. The eventual goal of all wealth builders is to lead the Cash Machine, not do the work themselves.

Building up the organization can be exciting, but it may also create uncertainty. Each employee or partner represents you and your business. It's important that you are clear about your *vision* and *values* so that you develop a consistent *culture* as you grow. This should be your approach with all your joint ventures as well.

As time went on and Marilyn got more comfortable with the Cash Machine, she could also work to increase her revenue and decrease her expenditures. Increasing revenue is a better emphasis when trying to grow, but expenditures need to be kept in check so that you can improve your margins. Marilyn also wanted to see if she would be better off being a high-end, low-volume business or a low-end, high-volume business. Eventually, she found that instead of managing a bunch of different contractors spending a lot of time on several different projects with several different clients, she wanted to focus on just a few large clients. This is a constantly managed process, and a lot of these answers surface during the first year of business.

Exit Strategies

You should always have an exit strategy in mind when you make an investment. Your Cash Machine will be one of your biggest investments, and as you future pace its path, you should consider what you want to see happen at the end of the day. There are several options.

Don't Exit

No exit is sometimes the best exit. If your Cash Machine is healthy and sustainable with little involvement from you, you can let it ride.

This is the perfect business, one that is running along with little maintenance—the proverbial cash cow. Get your children involved early; it will make any transition to them easier.

Acquisition

Though selling your company is one option, starting a company just to sell it is a big American myth. One problem with that strategy is the enormous capital gains tax you'll run into. Some businesses are cash-flow-producing machines. It wouldn't make any sense to sell such a business and take the tax consequences. *People don't live on buckets of cash; they live on cash flow.*

If your goal is to sell the company, you need to start with specific entities that will allow you to retain as much money as possible. You also need to create a strategy for immediately putting some of the money that you take out of the company into other, sustainable investments that will continue to create cash flow for you after you sell the company. This can be done through the Corporate Wealth Account. Eventually, you'll want to build the business to a target value that is much greater than you originally planned so that you can sustain your minimal cash-flow needs after the sale and after taxes. The strategy for sale starts at the beginning, and it's to create the entity structure; build the business; put some of the profits from the business into other investments; build the business; grow, grow, grow; then sell.

Strategic partners, competitors, suppliers—these are just some of the potential buyers for your Cash Machine. If selling your business is your goal all along, you should court these relationships early on. This might mean circling around a bigger player, like a little fly trying to get its attention, just so it knows you're there. You may be a nice purchase for it sometime down the road.

The payment for an acquisition can take the form of cash or stock, depending on your financial needs. Some Cash Machine owners choose to stay involved and play the fortunes of the new company by keeping their stake in stock. Others take the money and go. It depends on your plan and your Freedom Day goals.

If the company has run its course delivering cash flow and does not work as an ongoing concern, you may consider a *liquidation of assets,* if there are any.

IPO

Sometime in the 1990s, an initial public offering (IPO) became the Holy Grail. Going public—that is, offering shares of your company on a public exchange—has a good side and a bad side. The good is that it creates exposure. The bad is that it creates exposure. More good is that when the company goes public, it creates immediate cash value for the private shareholders. The bad is that the value of the stock itself will then fluctuate with the market's perception of the company—a perception to which the company is always vulnerable. Later on, in the mature life of your Cash Machine, consider talking to investor relations professionals about the pros and cons of both staying private and going public.

As the business grows, your skills will grow. As your skills grow, the business will grow. Managing and marketing your Cash Machine is a constant process of learning and expanding your world. Accelerate and never stop, and your wealth will do the same.

Teach your children well

CHAPTER TEN

The Kids' Cash Machine

The Next Generation of Millionaires

We all know that a lemonade stand is a lot of fun. But while we're at it, let's teach our children true entrepreneurship by teaching them how to build their own Cash Machine. This is the legacy and obligation of a Wealth Cycle: to teach the next generation. And to teach them correctly. The lemonade stand operator who sells 10 glasses of lemonade at $1 a glass and thinks he made $10 that day hasn't been taught about expenditures, profits, and losses. The young entrepreneur should know that he spent $12 to make the lemonade, sold it for $10, and so lost $2 that day. Not only is that realistic, but that type of learning will motivate most children to improve their situation.

Kids are more sophisticated these days. They understand technology, they are more aware of branding and marketing messages, and they often think in terms of business ideas and inventions. I'm sure you've seen this with many of the children in your world. My son Logan is that way. He knows all about our businesses and often asks me questions about our investments and our Cash Machines. One of his favorite things is collecting money out of the machines at the Laundromats we own. He also understands how that money is channeled into the LLC that owns the Laundromat and how a percentage of the revenue goes right for a monthly priority payment to the Corporate Wealth Account. Logan keeps an eye on that amount to see when we will have enough money to acquire or invest in our next business venture and keep the Wealth Cycle spinning.

Children have a lot of energy and a great capacity to absorb information and experiences. If they have the desire, encourage your child to pursue a Cash Machine, and support his or her efforts to do it correctly.

CASH MACHINE CASE IN POINT

Contracting the Collective

Alice Rose was a ninth grader who wanted to start her own business. She considered a newspaper delivery route, and through discussions with the boy down the street who had one, and some calculations, she realized that she could deliver 100 papers at 5 cents per delivery and make $5 a day, 5 days a week. This would be $25 every week and $100 a month. But she also realized, after talking to her model company (i.e., the neighbor), that this business would take her 45 minutes on a bike or an hour and 15 minutes if she walked. That was way too much time for her every morning.

Then she had an idea for a babysitting company. Alice had been babysitting since she was 12½, and so had two years of experience under her belt and a skill set upon which she could build a Cash Machine. But the other approaches to babysitting in her town did not make her think that babysitting could be a Cash Machine.

(continues)

(continued)

A friend of hers had made about three hundred dollars babysitting over the past three months. She asked her friend how she did it and priced it out for herself. If she charged $4.50 per hour, for two hours each day, three days a week, she would make $9 a day, $27 a week, and $108 a month. In three months she too would have over $300. She decided to devote Monday, Wednesday, and Friday to babysitting, if she could find the clients.

Many of the other kids in her class were babysitting, but most of them only had one or two jobs a month, and they had not expanded their clientele past their neighborhoods. They also found that it was difficult to get new clients beyond one or two degrees of personal reference.

That's when Alice had an idea. And thought of a better model.

Her uncle was a contractor, and she knew that he had different tradesmen, such as plumbers, electricians, and carpenters, who helped him build houses. Alice realized that while he said he built houses, he didn't really do it himself. This sounded good to her. She needed a hook to get babysitters and decided that she would tell them that they would (1) get time to do their homework, (2) learn parenting skills, (3) earn money, and (4) get more responsibility—without having to get the clients themselves or negotiate prices. A few people in her class signed up.

Now she needed clients. She asked a few parents what they thought the most important criteria for babysitters were and then incorporated these into her company name and tagline. Alice made flyers for the "Best of the Best Babysitters, the most reliable teens in town." She gave them to her babysitters to distribute throughout the neighborhood. She hired only babysitters who'd taken the babysitting safety and CPR class at the local Y, and she included this fact in her flyer. Alice also asked her parents for a loan of $50 and put a large display advertisement in the local paper. She already had a cell phone, and she made that the contact number, promising her parents that she would pay this phone bill herself as the Cash Machine got underway.

Talking her mother into joining her team to lend her name and age to help Alice create a limited liability company was the next step. Her mother became the company's legal managing member and bookkeeper. Soon Alice set up her entity structure and forecasting systems.

As a marketing angle, Alice thought of her aunt. She was a doctor and was often on call, even when she wasn't working. Alice decided to make it a point to have a few sitters on call, available at any time, night or day. The company soon gained a reputation for accessibility and last-minute scheduling, something that many busy parents were in great need of. Alice's business grew. Her pricing remained fair and competitive, and she increased her market share. She also doubled the number of her babysitters. She gave each sitter 70 percent of the fee, and took the rest for her company. By the time she went to college, Alice had expanded into other towns and handed the reins of the Cash Machine over to her younger brother.

This scenario is very reasonable. Creating a Cash Machine is just not that hard. It's also nice if you can teach the children in your life to build a business for a bigger purpose . . .

Charity Begins

I knew a young fifth grader named Douglas Jeremy who decided that he wanted to start a campaign to put small personal defibrillators in every school. He'd heard about a young kid in the county who had been hit hard with a soccer ball in a practice and died, and he realized that a defibrillator on site might have saved this child's life.

Douglas started a fund-raising campaign. It was slow going. He put jars at every school event, asking for a donation. It took him two months to raise $100, and he needed $5,000 for each machine. He also needed a better idea.

He decided to create a Cash Machine, the sole purpose of which would be to fund one defibrillator, with the hope of inspiring other communities to do the same. Douglas had done a lot of lawn work in his day, and his older brother had a painting crew after which he could model his business. His father was a lawyer, and he helped Douglas establish the company as a nonprofit organization under the school's nonprofit status.

And so Douglas created a lawn service business with six of his friends from school. They marketed it as a nonprofit company, with all the proceeds going to the defibrillator project, as they called it. They charged $5 an hour, and each kid did 5 hours of work a week, for $25 total. They raked and mowed lawns, clipped and weeded gardens, and even cleaned up trash. The six boys and girls collected $150 a week for four weeks straight.

Then four of the six kids who were helping him decided that they couldn't spend the time anymore. A natural entrepreneur, Douglas not only took it in stride, he decided to expand the business.

He called a reporter at the local newspaper and told him his idea. Then the reporter accompanied him as he went around to several of the businesses in his town and explained his services and the company's charitable mission. Douglas told the companies that he was creating a Corporate Clean-Up Marathon and asked if they would give a $6,000 donation to his cause, in return for which he would have at least a dozen kids show up at the office or store one day to do any cleaning or provide any service the employees or customers requested, such as cleaning desks and cubicles at the companies and carrying bags or helping select presents at the stores. The reporter promised to publicize the events. Two companies and one store in town thought that this sounded like fun and signed up.

Douglas put up a poster at school for an "as much as you can eat" ice cream sundae party, as well as a chance to get your picture in the newspaper—in exchange for spending one day next month at his Corporate Clean-Up Marathon. He got over 40 kids to sign up, and he spread them out to go to the companies after school, and to go to the store on the weekend.

In one month, Douglas had enough money for three defibrillators. He used the rest of the money to pay for the ice cream party, create T-shirts for all the kids who participated, and fund a campaign to get other groups of kids around the country interested in this cause.

This enterprise had elements of a Cash Machine in that it was built on a known skill set, was modeled after another business, was properly structured, used a team, and got experienced help. It also had a flexible plan, was cleverly marketed, generated cash immediately, and met the target revenue in short order. And, it had sustaining power.

Unlike traditional types of entrepreneurship, a Cash Machine is simple to start and sustain. It's based on *skills* that get you to an *idea* that is *modeled* after an established, successful business, with *Revenue Models* to hit specific projections, built on a *plan,* with a *team,* and *marketed, marketed, marketed.* That's it. The Cash Machine values action over theory, a realistic vision over lofty goals, skills over ideas, efficiency and expediency over perfection, money over method, and practice over pursuit. Any kid can and should do it. And with your help, they will.

Final Words

"Concerning all acts of initiative and creation, there is one elementary truth . . . that the moment one definitely commits oneself, then Providence moves too . . . whatever you can do or dream you can, begin it. Boldness has genius, power and magic in it. Begin it now."

Goethe

In seven weeks or less, a Cash Machine can and should be up and running. As you've seen, this approach to entrepreneurship is not that difficult, it's just different. Most of my clients have been able to take a skill set and turn it into a real live moneymaking venture. This money is created in weeks, if not days, and it is true cash, flowing steadily into your Wealth Cycle. I've seen it happen time after time, and if you follow the steps we've covered here, you too will have a moneymaking machine as part of your Millionaire Maker plan. With the entrepreneurial skill sets firmly in hand and a Cash Machine up and running and making you more and more money, you will be well on your way to fueling your Wealth Cycle and becoming a millionaire.

It begins with uncovering one's skills. Then a business idea is generated based on that skill set. The idea is modeled after similar businesses, and its potential is tested through revenue modeling. A plan is developed, the team is gathered, and then it's market, market, market. As the business grows and money is coming in, the entrepreneurial skill set of management, marketing, sales, operations, and finance kicks in.

Money is made and skills are learned. That's the Cash Machine. Once your entrepreneurship toolbox has been developed, you can take those skills to build another business, and then another, to generate more money and build more wealth.

The Cash Machine is an exciting building block in your Wealth Cycle. Start it today, and this will be a rewarding year for you. Your vision, your skills, your energy, your effort, and, most important, your persistence will be the key to a bigger, better life. It's just that good. Enjoy the abundance; it's there for you.

To your wealth

Index

About the Author

Loral Langemeier is the national bestselling author of *The Millionaire Maker* and *The Millionaire Maker's Guide to Wealth Cycle Investing*. A team-made millionaire and financial strategist, she is also a highly sought-after speaker and the founder of Live Out Loud, a coaching and seminar company that teaches her trademarked Wealth Cycle program (*www.liveoutloud.com*).